Frommer's®

Hong Kong
day BY day™

1st Edition

by Alex Ortolani

WILEY

Wiley Publishing, Inc.

Contents

Published by:

Wiley Publishing, Inc.

111 River St.
Hoboken, NJ 07030-5774

ISBN: 978-0-470-16544-7

Editor: Linda Barth
Production Editor: M. Faunette Johnston
Photo Editor: Richard Fox
Cartographer: Andrew Dolan
Production by Wiley Indianapolis Composition Services

For information on our other products and services or to obtain technical support, please contact our Customer Care Department within the U.S. at 800/762-2974, outside the U.S. at 317/572-3993 or fax 317/572-4002.

Wiley also publishes its books in a variety of electronic formats. Some content that appears in print may not be available in electronic formats.

Manufactured in China

5   4   3   2   1

A Note from the Publisher

Organizing your time. That's what this guide is all about.

Other guides give you long lists of things to see and do and then expect you to fit the pieces together. The Day by Day guides are different. These guides tell you the best of everything, and then they show you how to see it *in the smartest, most time-efficient way*. Our authors have designed detailed itineraries organized by time, neighborhood, or special interest. And each tour comes with a bulleted map that takes you from stop to stop.

Hoping to wander Hong Kong's narrow streets in search of some of the best market shopping in the world? Planning to experience Cantonese culture or explore the lingering British colonial influence? Whatever your interest or schedule, the Day by Days give you the smartest routes to follow. Not only do we take you to the top attractions, hotels, and restaurants, but we also help you access those special moments that locals get to experience— those "finds" that turn tourists into travelers.

The Day by Days are also your top choice if you're looking for one complete guide for all your travel needs. The best hotels and restaurants for every budget, the greatest shopping values, the wildest nightlife—it's all here.

Why should you trust our judgment? Because our authors personally visit each place they write about. They're an independent lot who say what they think and would never include places they wouldn't recommend to their best friends. They're also open to suggestions from readers. If you'd like to contact them, please send your comments my way at mspring@wiley.com, and I'll pass them on.

Enjoy your Day by Day guide—the most helpful travel companion you can buy. And have the trip of a lifetime.

Warm regards,

Michael Spring, Publisher
Frommer's Travel Guides

About the Author

Alex Ortolani worked as a journalist in Hong Kong and Beijing for over 3 years. He has master's degrees in creative writing and African literature and was a Fulbright scholar in South Africa.

Acknowledgments

Thanks to everyone in Hong Kong who helped me with the book, and to my friends and family for their support.

An Additional Note

Please be advised that travel information is subject to change at any time—and this is especially true of prices. We therefore suggest that you write or call ahead for confirmation when making your travel plans. The authors, editors, and publisher cannot be held responsible for the experiences of readers while traveling. Your safety is important to us, however, so we encourage you to stay alert and be aware of your surroundings.

Star Ratings, Icons & Abbreviations

Every hotel, restaurant, and attraction listing in this guide has been ranked for quality, value, service, amenities, and special features using a **star-rating system.** Hotels, restaurants, attractions, shopping, and nightlife are rated on a scale of zero stars (recommended) to three stars (exceptional). In addition to the star-rating system, we also use a **kids icon** to point out the best bets for families. Within each tour, we recommend cafes, bars or restaurants where you can take a break. Each of these stops appears in a shaded box marked with a coffee cup–shaped bullet.

The following **abbreviations** are used for credit cards:

AE	American Express	DISC	Discover	V	Visa
DC	Diners Club	MC	MasterCard		

Frommers.com

Now that you have this guidebook to help you plan a great trip, visit our website at **www.frommers.com** for additional travel information on more than 3,600 destinations. We update features regularly to give you instant access to the most current trip-planning information available. At Frommers. com, you'll find scoops on the best airfares, lodging rates, and car rental bargains. You can even book your travel online through our reliable travel booking partners. Other popular features include:

- Online updates of our most popular guidebooks
- Vacation sweepstakes and contest giveaways
- Newsletters highlighting the hottest travel trends
- Online travel message boards with featured travel discussions

A Note on Prices

In the "Take a Break" and "Best Bets" sections of this book, we have used a system of dollar signs to show a range of costs for 1 night in a hotel (the price of a double-occupancy room) or the cost of an entree at a restaurant. Use the following table to decipher the dollar signs:

Cost	Hotels	Restaurants
$	under $100	under $10
$$	$100–$200	$10–$20
$$$	$200–$300	$20–$30
$$$$	$300–$400	$30–$40
$$$$$	over $400	over $40

An Invitation to the Reader

In researching this book, we discovered many wonderful places—hotels, restaurants, shops, and more. We're sure you'll find others. Please tell us about them, so we can share the information with your fellow travelers in upcoming editions. If you were disappointed with a recommendation, we'd love to know that, too. Please write to:

Frommer's Hong Kong Day by Day, 1st Edition
Wiley Publishing, Inc. • 111 River St. • Hoboken, NJ 07030-5774

10 Favorite
Moments

10 Favorite **Moments**

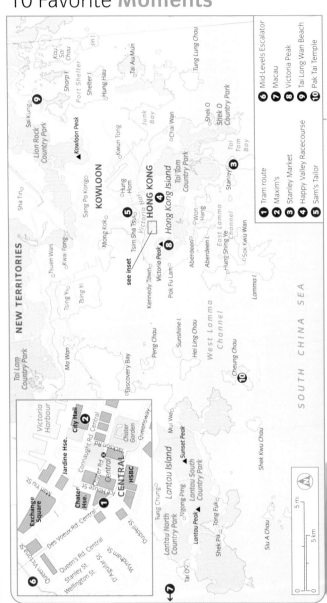

6 Mid-Levels Escalator
7 Macau
8 Victoria Peak
9 Tai Long Wan Beach
10 Pak Tai Temple

1 Tram route
2 Maxim's
3 Stanley Market
4 Happy Valley Racecourse
5 Sam's Tailor

Previous page: The Hong Kong skyline from Victoria Peak.

Hong Kong might have remained a sleepy fishing village had the Chinese not ceded control to the British during the opium wars of the mid-1800s. Instead, it rapidly grew into one of Asia's most vital trading and finance centers. But even under British rule, which ended in 1997, Hong Kong maintained much of its distinctly Chinese charm—the skyscrapers that sprouted along the shores of the South China Sea loom over Buddhist temples and goldfish markets. Today, the city offers a surprising blend of Eastern and Western culture, colonial influence, and Chinese tradition.

❶ Take a nostalgia trip on the trams. The double-decker trams that have been creeping along the northern edge of the island since 1904 are the ideal way to see the streets up close. Hong Kong natives use the trams to get around, but at only $HK2 a ride, they also offer one of the best tours of the city—from crumbling apartment blocks to dazzling skyscrapers—you're likely to find. *See p 152.*

❷ Start your day with dim sum at Maxim's Palace. Dim sum is a bit like tapas—lots of small plates served at once, generally for breakfast or lunch—and it's a Hong Kong specialty. Head to Maxim's Palace, which is one of the few places where dim sum is still delivered to diners on trolleys. You can choose from hundreds of dishes, but highlights are the squid tentacles, soup dumplings (*xiao long bao*), and barbecued pork buns (*char siu bau*). *See p 87.*

❸ Hike to Stanley Market. It goes without saying that you'll likely visit Stanley Market as it's a shopping mecca. But to get there, I suggest taking the road less traveled: Walk across the steep "Twins," the two hills that lead to Stanley from the north. The walk is challenging, but you'll be rewarded with outrageous views and that great Hong Kong rarity, a cool breeze. *See p 75.*

❹ Play the ponies. Horse racing may be the only activity that draws

A double-decker tram cruises along high-end shopping street Nathan Road at dusk.

people from all sectors of Hong Kong society together for a common purpose (seeing their horse win, of course). Join the crowds at Happy Valley Racecourse on a Wednesday night or Sha Tin on a Saturday and you'll feel like an honorary Hong Kong citizen. *See p 110.*

❺ Get custom fit. Over the years, Hong Kong and China's huge textile industry has encouraged the high-quality, inexpensive, personalized tailoring trade here. If you've never had a suit, dress, or shirt tailor-made before, Hong Kong's Tsim Sha Tsui is the place to indulge. Try Sam's for the best of the best. *See p 66.*

The Star Ferry passes in front of Hong Kong's cityscape, visible from Victoria Peak.

⑥ Ride the Mid-Levels escalator in the morning. Most visitors use the Mid-Levels escalator at night, when they're on their way to the restaurants, bars, and shops in Central and SoHo. But to get a sense of just how manic a city Hong Kong can be, take a ride on the escalator during the morning commute (6–10am), when it only runs downhill. *See p 7.*

⑦ Have dinner in Macau. Macau is a separate territory, once ruled by Portugal, and it has a wild flare all its own. Thanks to regular high-speed ferry service, you can get to Macau—a sort of Asian Las Vegas—in no time. You can have fantastic

A stone lion guards the entryway to the Pak Tai Temple on Cheung Chau.

Portuguese food, gamble, hear live music, and still be in bed in Hong Kong by midnight. *See p 130.*

⑧ Walk on the Peak. Victoria Peak (known simply as the Peak) is the tallest spot on Hong Kong Island and the observation platform at the top offers a stunning 360-degree view of the island, the territories, and the South China Sea. But the best way to experience the Peak is by going for a stroll (following Harlech and Lugard rds.). You'll see Hong Kong's sometimes-hidden natural beauty up close. *See p 7.*

⑨ Go to the beach. Hong Kong isn't known for its beaches, but it's hard to understand why. There are some truly gorgeous ocean-side spots here. Head to Tai Long Wan—a secluded, sandy beach in Sai Kung, also known as Big Wave Bay—for an afternoon and you'll feel like you've stumbled upon a hidden gem. *See p 70.*

⑩ Pray to the ancestors at Pak Tai Temple. Hong Kong's Buddhist temples are a reminder that there's life beyond work in this city. My favorite is Pak Tai Temple on Cheung Chau, where every year there's a festival to honor Pak Tai, the Taoist god of the sea. Like so many of Hong Kong's temples, it's an incense-laden oasis of serenity. *See p 140.* ●

The Best **in One Day**

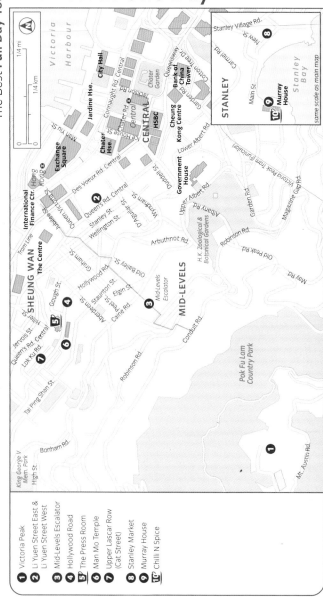

STANLEY

same scale as main map

- ❶ Victoria Peak
- ❷ Li Yuen Street East & Li Yuen Street West
- ❸ Mid-Levels Escalator
- ❹ Hollywood Road
- ❺ The Press Room
- ❻ Man Mo Temple
- ❼ Upper Lascar Row (Cat Street)
- ❽ Stanley Market
- ❾ Murray House
- 🍴 Chilli N Spice

Previous page: Buddhist monks pray at the Po Lin Monastery.

Hong Kong may be geographically small, but that doesn't mean it's easy to see in 1 day. If that's all you've got, I suggest you focus on taking in the city's striking natural beauty and exploring its world-famous markets. You'll get a sense of Hong Kong's vibrant East-meets-West way of life, and you'll likely find some inexpensive souvenirs along the way. START: **Peak Tram Station.**

❶ ★★★ Victoria Peak. At 396m (1,300 ft.), Victoria Peak is both Hong Kong's highest point and one of its ritziest neighborhoods. It also has the best view of the city thanks to its 360-degree open-air observatory. You can easily climb to the top, but for a quicker trip (and a major dose of nostalgia), take the Peak Tram, a funicular opened in 1888. 🕐 *90 min. Peak Tower.* ☎ *852/ 2849-7654. www.thepeak.com.hk. Peak Tram $HK22 adults, $HK8 kids. MTR: Central, exit J2. Bus: 15C from Central Pier Bus Terminus; 15 from Central Exchange Square.*

❷ ★ Li Yuen Street East and Li Yuen Street West. Welcome to the quintessential Hong Kong shopping experience: cheap goods in incredibly tight spaces. These two streets are lined with hawkers selling clothing, counterfeit designer handbags, and other inexpensive goods in tiny stalls filled to the brim with merchandise. 🕐 *30 min. Between Des Voeux Rd. and Queen's Rd. MTR: Central, exit C.*

❸ ★★★ Mid-Levels Escalator. Touted as the longest escalator in the world, this engineering marvel runs through Mid-Levels, a yuppie neighborhood terraced into the lower part of the Peak. The escalator—a combination of steps and ramps—passes through buildings and over streets lined with noodle shops and funky bars (Staunton St. is my favorite). You can get off to explore wherever you like. Be forewarned that if you plan to ride up the escalator, you must wait until after 10am— any earlier and the whole thing runs downhill for morning commuters. 🕐 *1 hr. MTR: Central, D2.*

❹ ★★ Hollywood Road. This wide, curving road is chock-full of shops and street vendors selling Chinese furniture, Tibetan rugs, Ming dynasty–era ceramic horses, sculptures of Chinese gods, and Maoist kitsch. It's the perfect place to pick up a uniquely Chinese souvenir: a statue of Kuan Ti, the god of war, to be put in your home to guard against intruders. 🕐 *1 hr. Exit Mid-Levels escalator at Hollywood Rd. Bus: 26.*

The Peak Tram runs every 10 to 15 minutes, from 7am to midnight.

A View from the Top

Don't expect an idyllic scene at the top of Victoria Peak. While the former governor's mansion's gardens are pretty and peaceful (the house was burned down by the Japanese during World War II), there's also a massive mall with overpriced shops, restaurants, and bars. It's a reminder that, despite its lovely scenery, Hong Kong is all about commerce these days. Still, one of the best parts of a Peak visit is getting to check out the city's astonishing skyline. To your right is the Wan Chai exhibition center jutting into the harbor, and farther east you'll see the bustling shopping neighborhood of Causeway Bay. To your left is Western Hong Kong, with its mix of residential buildings and shipping docks. Turn around and the city will seem like a distant memory—there's nothing but green rolling hills and the occasional mansion.

5 ★ **The Press Room.** Once the headquarters of the English-language *South China Morning Post*, this hip, atmospheric eatery has a large window overlooking the street. It also serves hearty, Asian-influenced Western cuisine, including a *fruits de mer* platter that offers a taste of some of Hong Kong's finest shellfish. *108 Hollywood Rd.* ☎ *852/2525-3444. $$$.*

6 ★★★ **Man Mo Temple.** Hong Kong's oldest temple was built well before the British arrived in 1841, though the exact date is a mystery. It's dedicated to the gods of literature and war (Man and Mo); the grand entrance is flanked by stone lions for protection. Inside, amid statues of Man, Mo, and other gods, ashes flutter from the huge, curling incense sticks that hang from the ceiling—the smoke is intended to carry prayers to heaven—as the Buddhist faithful pray to their ancestors. ⏱ *30 min. Hollywood Rd. and Ladder St.* ☎ *852/2803-2916. Free admission. Daily 8am–6pm. MTR: Sheung Wan, exit A2. Bus: 26.*

7 ★ **Upper Lascar Row (Cat Street).** The nickname Cat Street comes from this shopping area's dodgy past, when it was known as a market for stolen goods. In Cantonese slang, thieves are "rats," and the people who buy from them are

Mao alarm clocks for sale along Hollywood Road. See p 8.

A brass lion guards an altar at Man Mo Temple.

Central, but it was taken apart and moved here to make way for the Bank of China tower. After a few mishaps (somehow in piecing it back together, the construction crew ended up with six extra columns, which stand between the building and the water), it's back in one piece. It now has a small exhibition on its history on the ground floor and shops and restaurants on the floors above. ⏱ *40 min. Stanley Plaza. Restaurant, bar, and shop hours vary. Hong Kong Maritime Museum* ☎ *852/2813-2322. www. hkmaritimemuseum.org. Admission $HK20 adults; $HK10 kids. Tues–Fri & Sun 10am–6pm; Sat 10am–7pm. Bus: 6, 6A, 6X, or 260.*

"cats." Though you probably won't play the role of feline on this street nowadays, you'll most likely overpay no matter how sly you are. But with calligraphy brushes, Mao pins, and other souvenirs on offer starting at $HK40, it still won't set you back much. ⏱ *30 min. Upper Lascar Row. MTR: Sheung Wan, exit A2. Bus: 26. See p 65.*

8 ★★ **Stanley Market.** The journey out of the heart of downtown to this crowded market is worth the trip, even if you're not in the mood for more shopping. En route to Stanley, you'll be treated to outstanding views of Hong Kong's open hillsides and ocean vistas. Unfortunately, most experienced shoppers will tell you goods are overpriced at the market itself. I suggest heading for the waterfront, which is lined with restaurants and bars. ⏱ *3 hr. Bus: 6, 6A, 6X, or 260 from Central Exchange Square bus terminal; 973 from Mody Rd. in Tsim Sha Tsui East or from Canton Rd. in Tsim Sha Tsui. See p 65.*

9 **Murray House.** Built in 1848, this is one of Hong Kong's oldest colonial buildings. It used to be in

10P Of all the food options in Stanley, **Chilli N Spice** offers the best combo package—excellent Asian fusion cuisine, balcony seating overlooking the water, and a loungelike atmosphere. The bar has a wide selection of Asian beers to go with inventive entrees like Singaporean-style fried curry crab, Indonesian curry chicken, and fried beef filet with mango and chili. *Shop 101, Murray House.* ☎ *852/2899-0147. $$.*

Be prepared to haggle along Cat Street.

The Best **in Two Days**

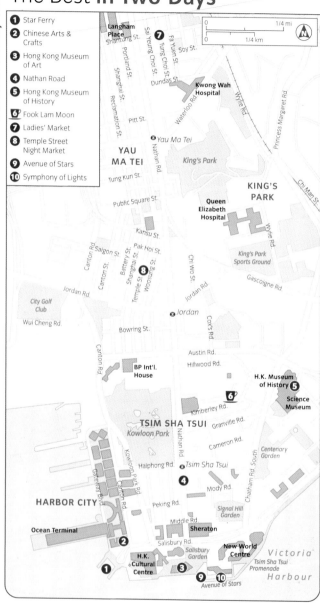

1 Star Ferry
2 Chinese Arts & Crafts
3 Hong Kong Museum of Art
4 Nathan Road
5 Hong Kong Museum of History
6 Fook Lam Moon
7 Ladies' Market
8 Temple Street Night Market
9 Avenue of Stars
10 Symphony of Lights

O n your second day, head to Kowloon for a chance to see life in the heart of Cantonese Hong Kong. Kowloon is better known for arts and entertainment than for its markets and skyscrapers. It's the best part of town in which to soak up the local atmosphere. START: **Central Ferry Pier.**

① ★★★ **Star Ferry.** The Star Ferry has been running since 1898, and until a tunnel opened in 1972, it was the primary mode of transportation for people crossing the harbor. It's definitely worth splurging for the upper deck (the lower deck is cheaper) for a better view as you chug toward Kowloon. The trip is very quick (you're only on the water for about 5 min.), so make sure you have your camera ready. ⏱ *30 min. Central Pier, Tsim Sha Tsui terminal.* ☎ *852/2367-7065. www.starferry. com.hk. $HK2.20 upper deck; children $HK1.30. Daily 6:30am–11:30pm. MTR: Central, exit K.*

② ★ **Chinese Arts & Crafts.** This is my favorite place to shop for upscale Chinese arts and crafts. This store (the main, and best, branch of a chain) offers everything from elegant silk clothing to paintings, tea sets, and even herbal medicine. It's

An exhibit on Cantonese opera at the Museum of History illustrates how performers prepare for a show. See p 12.

Traditional Chinese silks for sale at Chinese Arts & Crafts

also one of the most reliable places to buy jade, which can be tricky to shop for as quality varies widely. The prices are high, but you'll get what you pay for. ⏱ *45 min. 3 Salisbury Rd.* ☎ *852/2735-4061. www. crcretail.com. Daily 10am–9:30pm. MTR: Tsim Sha Tsui, exit E. See p 61.*

③ ★★ **Hong Kong Museum of Art.** The exterior is a beige monstrosity, and the interior feels a bit like a high school library, but don't be fooled—the artwork, ranging from modern Chinese painting to Neolithic bronzes, makes this museum worth a visit. My favorite is the permanent exhibit on the history of Hong Kong, which includes old photographs that show just how much the city has changed. ⏱ *2 hr. Hong Kong Cultural Centre Complex, 10 Salisbury Rd.*

Shop Smart

Since so much of the Hong Kong experience involves market shopping, it's worth sharing a few insider tips. This being Asia, sizes tend to run small, but don't be dismayed if you can't find an XL—just ask, as merchants tend to keep additional sizes and colors stashed away for such occasions. And definitely don't be afraid to bargain with market vendors; it's considered a normal part of shopping here. The rule of thumb is to offer a quarter of what the seller is asking, and then try not to settle for more than half of the original price. If you're not happy with the final price, walk away. Unless you've stumbled upon a must-have antique or some truly unique jewelry, you'll likely see similar, if not identical, goods at the next market you visit.

☎ 852/2721-0116. www.hk.art. museum. Admission $HK10 adults; free for kids under 4. Free Wed. Mon–Wed, Fri 10am–6pm; Sat 10am–8pm; Thurs closed. MTR: Tsim Sha Tsui, exit E. See p 29.

④ ★ **Nathan Road.** Also known as the Golden Mile, this is Kowloon's major artery and the closest thing Hong Kong has to New York City's Fifth Avenue. The overwhelming

A fortuneteller gives a reading at the Temple Street Night Market.

number of neon signs alone makes it worth a stop. If you're in the market for a tailored suit, this is the place to come. Don't feel pressured by the salespeople—take your time and seek out the fabrics and styles you like best. ⏱ 1 hr. MTR: Tsim Sha Tsui, exit A1.

⑤ ★★★ **Hong Kong Museum of History.** This huge, lively museum takes you chronologically through Hong Kong's history. Exhibits include replicas of pre-British-era homes, as well as a full-size model of a streetcar of the type used in Central around 1881. You'll learn everything you need to know about the opium wars, the Japanese occupation during World War II, and the 1997 hand over from Great Britain to China. ⏱ 1 hr. 100 Chatham Rd., South. ☎ 852/2724-9042. www.lcsd. gov.hk/hkmh. Admission $HK10 adults; free for kids under 4. Wed free. Mon–Fri 9:30am–12:30pm, 2:30–5pm; Sat 9:30am–noon. MTR: Tsim Sha Tsui, exit B2. Bus: 5 or 5C from Star Ferry terminal. See p 29.

⑥ ★★ **Fook Lam Moon.** Founded in 1948, this restaurant (now part of a small chain) serves the best classic Cantonese dishes in Hong Kong, including braised shark's fin with brown sauce, goose web, roast suckling pig, and braised abalone. The decor is a bit outdated, but with food this good, who cares? *53–59 Kimberley Rd., Shop 8, 1st Floor.* ☎ *852/2366-0286. $$.*

⓻ ★ Ladies' Market. As the name suggests, this market once specialized in ladies' clothing. Now it sells pretty much everything. Here you'll find "rip-offs" of brand names (who needs a pricey Rolex watch when you can buy a Lorex for next to nothing?) alongside everyday goods from lamps to apple peelers. Just keep in mind that even if you get a good price, the quality is likely to be as dubious as the label. *1 hr. MTR: Mongkok, D3. See p 65.*

A bronze statue of kung fu film star Bruce Lee looms over Avenue of Stars.

Shoppers check out goods at the Ladies' Market.

⓼ ★★★ Temple Street Night Market. Temple Street, which doesn't get going until after 4pm, is worth a stop even if you're shopped out. The big draw is the dai pai dong stalls selling everything from hairy crab to crispy fried chicken. All of it is delicious. Cantonese opera singers sometimes hold mini-concerts on the street, and fortunetellers, many of whom speak English, will read your future for a price (again, bargain). *2 hr. Salisbury Rd.* ☎ *852/2920-2888. MTR: Jordan, C2. See p 65.*

⓽ ★★★ Avenue of Stars. Avenue of Stars was a $HK40-million project opened in 2004 to honor Hong Kong's film industry. It's a lot like the scene along Hollywood's Walk of Fame—there are stars for such local legends as director Wong Kar-wai and actors Jet Li and Maggie Cheung. There's also a statue of karate-legend Bruce Lee. *30 min. Avenue of Stars. MTR: Tsim Sha Tsui, exit G. Star Ferry terminal in Tsim Sha Tsui.*

⓾ Symphony of Lights. At 8pm every night 30 buildings on either side of the harbor participate in a massive 20-minute light-and-laser show coordinated to music. It is as unusual as it sounds, and worth checking out. You'll get the best view from the Avenue of Stars. *20 min. Avenue of Stars. MTR: Tsim Sha Tsui, exit G. Star Ferry terminal in Tsim Sha Tsui.*

The Best **in Three Days**

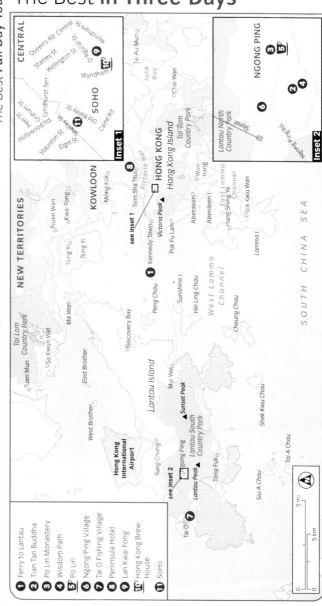

1 Ferry to Lantau
2 Tian Tan Buddha
3 Po Lin Monastery
4 Wisdom Path
5 Po Lin
6 Ngong Ping Village
7 Tai O Fishing Village
8 Peninsula Hotel
9 Lan Kwai Fong
10 Hong Kong Brew House
11 SoHo

CENTRAL

Queen's Rd Central
Stanley St.
Wellington St.
D'Aguilar St.
Wyndham St.
9
Wyndham

Lyndhurst Terr.
Peel St.
Graham St.
Old Bailey St.
Hollywood Rd.
Staunton St.
Shelley St.
Caine Rd.
Elgin St.
11

SOHO

Inset 1

NGONG PING
3
5
2
4
6

Lantau North
Country Park

Ngong Ping Rd
Skyrail

Inset 2

NEW TERRITORIES

Tai Lam
Country Park

Tuen Mun
So Kwun Wat
Ma Wan
Tsuen Wan
Kwai Fong
Tsing Yi
Tsing Yi

KOWLOON

Mong Kok
Tai Au Mun
Junk
Bay
Chai Wan
Victoria Hbr.
Tsim Sha Tsui
8

see inset 1

HONG KONG
Kennedy Town
Victoria Peak
Hong Kong Island
Pok Fu Lam

Tai Tam
Country Park

East Brother
West Brother

Hong Kong International Airport

Discovery Bay

Peng Chau

Sunshine I.

Hei Ling Chau

West Lamma
Channel

Cheung Chau

Mu Wo
Lantau Island

Ngong Ping
Lantau South
Country Park
Lantau Peak
Sunset Peak

Tung Chung
see inset 2

Tai O
7

Tong Fuk

Siu A Chau

Shek Kwu Chau

Tai A Chau

Aberdeen
Aberdeen I.
Wong
Chuk
Hang

Chung Shing Ye

Sok Kwu Wan

Lamma I.

East Lamma
Channel

SOUTH CHINA SEA

N

5 mi

5 km

For your third day, head out of the city proper and see what Hong Kong has to offer besides narrow streets and crowded markets. You'll get a little spiritual with the giant Buddha on Lantau, enjoy a slightly cheesy Chinese village theme park, and end by exploring Lan Kwai Fong and SoHo, the two main hot spots for Hong Kong's nightlife. You'll come away with a deep understanding of why the phrase "East meets West" is nearly always used when talking about Hong Kong. START: **Ferry terminal in Central.**

❶ ★★ Ferry to Lantau. Hop on the ferry to Lantau—the terminal you'll depart from is clearly marked. Just make sure you take one of the fast ferries. If you take one of the slow boats, you'll end up with way more time gazing at Hong Kong's skyline than you probably want or need, and you'll lose valuable time from the rest of your very busy day. ⏱ *1 hr. Ferry Pier no. 6. Admission Mon–Sat $HK16; Sun $HK25. Exact change needed.*

❷ ★★★ Tian Tan Buddha. Tour guides claim this is the world's largest seated bronze Buddha, and it does look massive, even from the bottom of the 260 steep steps it takes to reach it. Built in 1993, the Buddha is 31m (102 ft.) high and weighs 250 tons. He also has a fantastic view of Lantau from 750m (2,460 ft.) above sea level. There is a small museum inside the statue, but there's not much to see. The ticket price includes lunch at the Po Lin Monastery (see "Po Lin Monastery" below). ⏱ *2 hr. Admission $HK60 includes regular lunch; $HK100 includes deluxe lunch. Daily 10am–6pm. Bus: 2 from Mui Wo Pier.*

The Tian Tan Buddha looks out over the island of Lantau.

Transportation City

Hong Kong, as you'll quickly notice, has a slightly ridiculous range of transportation options. These include taxis, buses, the subway (MTR), ferries, wooden trams, minibuses, junks, and sampans for hire. It's no wonder many residents have never driven a car. In this book, we list MTR stops, which often require a bit of walking, as well as bus routes and ferries when necessary. While we normally recommend public transportation, taking cheap, fast taxis around Central may be your best option if you have limited time. If you're staying in Hong Kong more than 5 days, get a pre-paid Octopus card (see "Getting Around," p 151 for more information), which can be swiped in most every form of public transport.

One of the many statues of Chinese gods that adorn a temple at the Po Lin Monastery.

Having lunch at the 5 **Po Lin Monastery** is a real treat. You'll buy a timed ticket either at the base of the Buddha (if you're planning to visit) or at the monastery itself. I suggest opting for the regular lunch, which is served family style (big helpings of vegetables, soups, and rice are brought to the table for all to share) in a colorful dining room packed with Chinese families. You can also opt for the deluxe lunch, which is served on plates in a quieter room filled mostly with tourists. *Ngong Ping.* ☎ 852/2895-5248. $

3 ★ **Po Lin Monastery.** This monastery was founded more than 100 years ago by reclusive Buddhist monks; the remaining structures date from 1921 and 1970. The largest temple at Po Lin (which means "precious lotus") has a golden roof and three bronze statues of the Buddha representing the past, present, and future. As you wander the grounds, you'll see monks going about their daily routine. 45 min. Ngong Ping. ☎ 852/2895-5248. www.plm.org.hk/blcs/en/index.asp. Daily 10am–6pm. Bus: 2 from Mui Wo Pier.

4 ★ **Wisdom Path.** Stroll down the Wisdom Path, which leads to a figure eight of 38 wooden pillars engraved with quotes from the *Heart Sutra*. The *Heart Sutra* is a text read by Confucians, Buddhists, and Taoists, and it includes mantras describing the philosophies of wisdom, compassion, and enlightenment. The site was built in 2005 and is intended to promote peace and tranquility. 45 min. Wisdom Path, Ngong Ping. www.tourism.gov.hk/english/current/current_heart.html.

6 kids **Ngong Ping Village.** This relatively new tourist spot offers a bit of Chinese culture and history in a Disneyland-style setting. The *Walking with Buddha* attraction tells the story of Siddhartha Gautama, the young prince who attained enlightenment and became Buddha. The *Monkey's Tale Theatre* is a high-tech computer-animated retelling of the traditional Buddhist story of the Monkey King. Best of all is a Chinese tea ceremony, which offers an inside look at this age-old custom along with a history of the

The Wisdom Path was laid out in a figure eight to symbolize infinity.

The Monastery and the Buddha

Po Lin Monastery was founded more than 100 years ago by three Zen masters, Da Yue, Dun Xiu, and Yue Ming, who arrived in Lantau from Zhejiang in mainland China. They felt the area, nestled amid mountains, would be perfect for a monastery and eventually monks from southern China were drawn to the quiet beauty of the place. The big Buddha went up on neighboring Muk Yue Peak in 1993, bringing with it an influx of visitors, though the monks don't seem to mind. As for the Buddha, he sits cross-legged (the real Buddha was said to be seated cross-legged when he achieved enlightenment) and his right hand is raised in a vow to eliminate suffering from all beings on Earth. His left hand rests on his thigh with the palm up, as a symbol of Buddha's compassion in granting happiness to all people. The icon on his chest—which will unfortunately remind Westerners of a swastika—represents the everlasting presence and compassion of the Buddha.

role tea has played in Chinese culture. ⏱ *1 hr.* ☎ *852/2109-9898. Free admission to village. Admission to Walking with Buddha and Monkey's Tale Theatre each HK$35 adults; $HK18 kids. Combination ticket for both shows $HK65 adults; $HK35 kids. Mon–Fri 10am–6pm; Sat–Sun 10am–6:30pm.*

❼ ★★ Tai O Fishing Village.
Located on the far western coast of Lantau, this fishing village is known as the "Venice of Hong Kong" thanks to the traditional stilt housing found here. Though some of its charm has been lost to development, you can still see local fisherfolk going out for the day's catch. For a small fee, you can usually catch a short fishing boat ride along the coast—if you're lucky, you may see Chinese white dolphins. If you'd rather stay landlocked, head for the shops, where you can pick up a jar of shrimp paste, a pungent sauce made by fermenting shrimp in spices in the sun. ⏱ *1hr. Tai O Fishing Village. Bus from Ngong Ping.*

❽ ★★★ The Peninsula Hotel.
This Hong Kong landmark has a storied history in the city. Opened in 1928, it is the territory's oldest existing hotel. Once located at the end of the trans-Siberian railroad, the Peninsula became known as a place for the wealthy and famous to stay when traveling in Asia—the place even rents out its own

A traditional Chinese gateway at the Ngong Ping village.

Stilt houses line the shores at the Tai O fishing village. See p 17.

Rolls-Royces. As the years passed, having afternoon tea in the Peninsula's posh lobby became a must for Hong Kong visitors. ⏱ 1 hr. Salisbury Rd. ☎ 852/2920-2888. MTR: Tsim Sha Tsui, exit E. See p 126.

⑨ ★★ Lan Kwai Fong. Walking up D'Aguillar Street into the heart of Lan Kwai Fong at night is a bit like walking into a street festival. Crowds of people unwind from the daily grind, basically by drinking in the street. It's a lot more fun than it sounds—it's one of the most lively bar scenes you're likely to find anywhere. *MTR: Central. Bus: 26.*

Of all the pubs in this area, my personal favorite is the **⑩ Hong Kong Brew House.** A cavernous place with a patio out front, it has a great beer selection. Even better, if you come early, you can nab a seat outside, where you'll have a prime spot for observing Lan Kwai Fong's Mardi Gras–style nightlife. Stop by for one of the microbrews (I recommend the Aldridge Pale Ale or the Hong Kong Lager) and watch the madness unfold. *33 Wyndham St.* ☎ *852/2522-5559. $*

⑪ ★★★ SoHo (South of Hollywood). While Lan Kwai Fong (LKF) is the international face of Hong Kong's nightlife, bars, and clubs, the area known as SoHo, located south of LKF, has some of the best offerings. The scene is a bit less of, well, a scene than in LKF, and you'll find a funkier crowd here. It's the place to head if you'd like a less frat-partyish atmosphere. See chapter 7, "The Best Nightlife," for more information on the clubs and bars here. *MTR: Central. Bus: 26.* ●

Double-decker wooden trams are just one of many options for making your way around Hong Kong.

Chinese Hong Kong

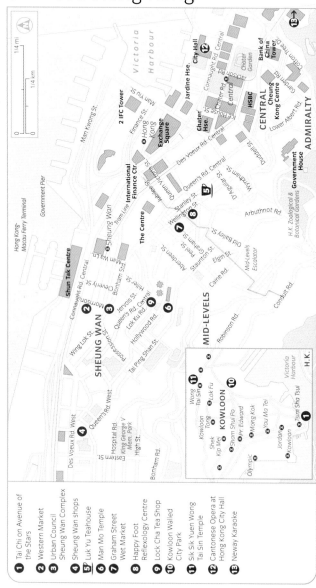

Previous page: Massive coils of incense in Man Mo Temple.

Hong Kong means "fragrant harbor" in Cantonese. At one time, that fragrance was pleasant, but like so many things here, that too has changed, thanks to industrialization and population growth. Perhaps the one thing that's remained the same is the fact that at its core, Hong Kong is a Chinese city. That will seem obvious to anyone wandering the bustling streets of Mongkok or stopping into the shopping malls of Causeway Bay, but this tour gives you a look at the more historic heart of Chinese Hong Kong. START: **MTR to Avenue of Stars, Tsim Sha Tsui.**

❶ ★ Tai Chi on the Avenue of Stars. You've probably heard of tai chi, a martial art that looks like a kind of shadowboxing. Tai chi is hugely popular, especially with older Chinese, and you'll see people practicing it in parks all over Hong Kong. The Hong Kong Tourism Board offers free classes for beginners 4 days a week; the best is at the Avenue of Stars in Tsim Sha Tsui, where there's a view of the skyline. ⏱ *1 hr.* ☎ *852/2508-1234. www.hktourism-board.com. To check the dates and make a reservation, call the tourism board. MTR: Tsim Sha Tsui.*

❷ ★★★ Western Market. Construction of this massive, Edwardian-style market building was finished in 1906, and it was used as a food market until 1988. Now it's a historic landmark and, not surprisingly in this shopping-crazed city, a market for souvenirs. You can pick up things like Chinese seals and jade on the first floor and check out the bright bolts of silk on the second floor. The top floor is home to The Grand Stage, which features ballroom dancing from 2:30 to 6pm daily. ⏱ *30 min. 323 Des Voeux Rd., Central. Daily 10am–7pm. MTR: Sheung Wan.*

❸ Urban Council Sheung Wan Complex. This complex is one of Hong Kong's largest neighborhood markets. The ground floor features fish and poultry, the first floor features meats and vegetables, and the top floor has a large food hall. The Chinese value fresh food—and I do mean fresh. Live chickens are killed on the spot and tossed into machines that pluck their feathers (though for health reasons, live chickens are to be banned from wet markets by 2009), and you may see baskets filled with the discarded horns and skulls of bulls.

The Chinese consider tai chi to be exercise for the mind as well as for the body.

Dried fish for sale along Des Voeux Rd in Sheung Wan.

This is not a stop for the faint of heart, but it is a fascinating look at Chinese culture. *Morrison St. and Bonham Strand, Central. Daily 6am–8pm. MTR: Sheung Wan.*

❹ Sheung Wan Shops. Sheung Wan is an area that's home to Chinese wholesale businesses—many of them family run—that have been here for decades. Stroll Des Voeux Road to see the dried seafood shops selling everything from scallops to seaweed and Ko Shing Street

for Chinese herbal medicine dealers (see "Chinese Medicine," p 51). My personal favorite is Queen's Road West, where you'll find shops selling red paper offerings that the Chinese traditionally burn to honor the dead. *90 min. MTR: Sheung Wan.*

❺ ★★★ Luk Yu Teahouse. Serving tea and dim sum since 1933, Luk Yu is considered Hong Kong's most authentic remaining teahouse,

Dim Sum

When it comes to Cantonese cuisine, dim sum is as good as it gets. Traditionally served for breakfast or lunch, diners choose from loads of small dishes that are meant to be shared—it's the Chinese version of tapas. In the past, dim sum was served from trolley carts; waiters rolled the offerings past the table for you to pick and choose. These days, it's more likely that you'll check off what you want on a paper menu. Below is a very short list of some of the classic dishes you should make sure to try:

char siu bau—steamed barbecue pork buns
cheung fun—steamed rice flour rolls with shrimp, beef, or pork
chun gun—fried spring rolls
fan guo—steamed dumplings with shrimp and bamboo shoots
fu pei gun—crispy bean-curd rolls
fung jau—fried chicken's feet
loh mei fan—sticky rice wrapped in lotus leaf
pai guat—small braised spareribs with black beans
siu mai—steamed pork and shrimp dumplings

complete with ceiling fans, spittoons, and waiters who look as if they've been around since the place opened. It's always crowded with regulars—a sure sign that the food is good. The English-language menu doesn't list all of the options available, so ask your waiter for help. Come before 11am to have dim sum served the old-fashioned way—off trolleys. *24–26 Stanley St.* ☎ *852/2523-5464. $$$.*

Enormous coils of incense at the Man Mo Temple. The smoke is believed to carry prayers to heaven.

⑥ ★★ Man Mo Temple. Dating back to the 1840s, this is Hong Kong's oldest temple. Man is the god of literature and Mo is the god of war—he's also the special protector of police, and shrines to him can be found in police stations all over the city. Look for the two ornately carved sedan chairs that date to the 1800s and were used to carry statues of the two gods through the streets during festivals. You'll also notice the massive coils of incense that hang from the ceiling—they can burn as long as 3 weeks. ⏱ *45 min. Hollywood Rd. and Ladder St.* ☎ *852/2803-2916. Daily 8am–6pm. Free admission. Bus: 26. See p 8, bullet ⑥.*

⑦ ★★ Graham Street Wet Market. This is not your average food shopping experience. As you walk past the stalls along this narrow street, you'll find yourself surrounded by tanks of live fish, crustaceans, and even turtles. Be brave and try the Cantonese "hundred-year" eggs, which are chicken, duck, or quail eggs that have been soaked in a mixture of salt, lime, clay, and rice straw for several weeks. Surprisingly, these dark green eggs aren't terribly flavorful on their own (which may not be a bad thing), but they're excellent when served with dipping sauce. ⏱ *45 min. Graham St. MTR: Central, D2 to Mid-Levels escalator. Bus: 26.*

In addition to food and Chinese medicine, you'll find souvenirs like Cantonese opera headgear in Sheung Wan.

Walled In

The relatively new Kowloon Walled City Park took the place of what had been one of Hong Kong's most notorious neighborhoods. Originally, this spot was right on the water (thanks to reclamation—the use of landfill to expand the city—it's now inland), which is why the Chinese built a fort here to defend Kowloon against the British, who had already taken Hong Kong. The fort didn't really do the job, but China held onto it after Kowloon fell in 1898. Ignored by British authorities, the area within the fort's walls became a poor, dangerous warren of narrow alleys and crumbling homes. And because it wasn't subject to British law, the "walled city" was a thriving hub of illegal activity. At one point, the only form of law enforcement came from the triads—gangs that still operate many of Hong Kong's nightclubs and saunas. But despite the walled city's reputation, many people lived ordinary, if unglamorous lives here. In 1994 the place was razed to make way for Kowloon Walled City Park.

❽ ★★ Happy Foot Reflexology Centre. After so much walking, it's time for a very Asian remedy for tired feet: a foot massage. Although Hong Kong has too many spa options to count, the quality varies. I recommend Happy Foot because their reflexologists are consistently excellent and the prices are reasonable (starting at $HK198 for 50 min.). The Chinese believe that when a skilled foot reflexologist goes to work, he or she is not just giving your toes a rubdown, but is specifically

Hundred-year eggs on display at the Graham Street Wet Market.

targeting pressure points that correspond to the rest of your body. ⏱ *1 hr. 98–102 Wellington St. Daily 10am–midnight. MTR: Central, exit D2.*

❾ ★★★ Lock Cha Tea Shop. Tea is a staple of Chinese life, and the Lock Cha Tea Shop, with its traditional Chinese furniture and comprehensive stock of over 100 types of tea, is the place to go for it. Here, you can pick up flavors like jasmine green and peony white, both from Fujian province. If you're having trouble choosing, the staff will not only help you navigate the myriad choices, but will show you the proper way to pour. The shop also sells tea sets and snacks. ⏱ *30 min. 290b Queen's Rd.* ☎ *852/2805-1360. Daily 11am–7pm.*

❿ ★★ Kowloon Walled City Park. This park was designed to re-create the style of a classical Southern Chinese garden, and you can follow its winding paths past bonsai, bamboo, ponds, and streams. The landscaping and the Chinese zodiac

Worshippers gather to burn incense and pray at the Wong Tai Sin Temple.

sculpture garden are impressive and so is the area's history (see "Walled In," above). The park occupies what was once a Chinese fort, built in 1847; its history is recounted in a photography exhibit at a former almshouse. ⏱ *2 hr. Tung Tsing Rd. MTR: Lok Fu, exit B. Bus: 1, 10, or 113.*

⓫ ★★ Sik Sik Yuen Wong Tai Sin Temple.

This busy Taoist temple honoring Wong Tai Sin, the god of healing, is actually a collection of temples set amid peaceful gardens and fountains. The altar of the main building features a painting of Wong, a young shepherd who Taoists believe disappeared only to return decades later with incredible healing powers. People now pray to him not only for physical well-being, but also for health in relationships and business dealings. ⏱ *45 min. Lung Cheung Rd. www.siksikyuen. org.hk. Daily 7am–5:30pm. MTR: Wong Tai Sin, exit B2.*

⓬ ★★ Cantonese Opera at Hong Kong City Hall.

Cantonese opera may strike you as one of the stranger relics of China's past. The costumes are elaborate, and the lyrics are sung in a shrill, high-pitched tone that is often bracing to Western ears. Don't be embarrassed to leave midway through—performances can be long, and you won't be the only one doing so. Check the listings at Hong Kong City Hall and get your tickets in advance, as shows often sell out. *5 Edinbugh Place.* ☎ *852/2111-5999. www.lcsd.gov.hk/hkch. Tickets start at $HK100. MTR: Central.*

⓭ ★ Neway Karaoke.

Karaoke is a Japanese invention, but it's hugely popular in Hong Kong. Some locals will even admit to practicing at home so they can put on a better performance in public. My favorite spot to let loose at the end of a long day is the Neway Karaoke Box where you can choose from a huge selection of songs. If you're feeling shy, request one of the private rooms. *Causeway Bay Plaza, 489 Hennesy Rd, 3rd floor.* ☎ *852/2196-2196. www.newaykb.com. MTR: Causeway Bay, exit E.*

A sign for Happy Foot Massage illustrates pressure points on the feet that correspond to the rest of the body.

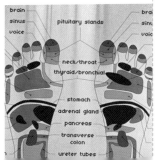

The Best Museums & Galleries

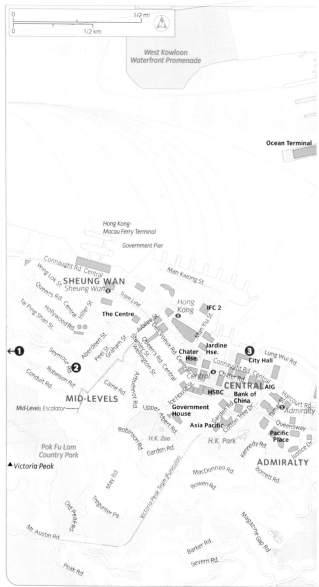

0 _____ 1/2 mi
0 _____ 1/2 km

West Kowloon
Waterfront Promenade

Ocean Terminal

Hong Kong-
Macau Ferry Terminal

Government Pier

Connaught Rd. Central

Man Kwong St.

Wing Lok St.
Queen's Rd. Central

SHEUNG WAN
Sheung Wan

Tram Line

Tai Ping Shan St.

Hollywood Rd.

The Centre

Hong
Kong

IFC 2

Man Yiu St.

Hiller St.

Aberdeen St.

Peel St.

Graham St.

Jubilee St.

Stevenson St.

Wellington St.

Queen's Rd. Central

Des Voeux Rd. Central

**Jardine
Hse.**

**Chater
Hse.**

City Hall

Lung Wui Rd.

Connaught Rd. Central/

←**❶**

Seymour St.

❷

Robinson Rd.

Conduit Rd.

Caine Rd.

Arbuthnot Rd.

Central

❸ Chater Rd.

CENTRAL AIG

Chater Rd. Central/

Harcourt Rd.

MID-LEVELS

Mid-Levels Escalator

Upper Albert Rd.

**Government
House**

HSBC

**Bank of
China**

Garden Rd.

Cotton Tree Dr.

Tamar

❸ **Admiralty**

Queensway

**Pacific
Place**

Justice Dr.

Robinson Rd.

Asia Pacific

H.K. Zoo

Garden Rd.

H.K. Park

Kennedy Rd.

ADMIRALTY

Pok Fu Lam
Country Park

▲Victoria Peak

Man Rd.

Tregunter Pa.

Victoria Peak Tram (Funicular)

MacDonnell Rd.

Bowen Rd.

Borrett Rd.

Magazine Gap Rd.

Old Peak Rd.

Mt. Austin Rd.

Barker Rd.

Severn Rd.

Peak Rd.

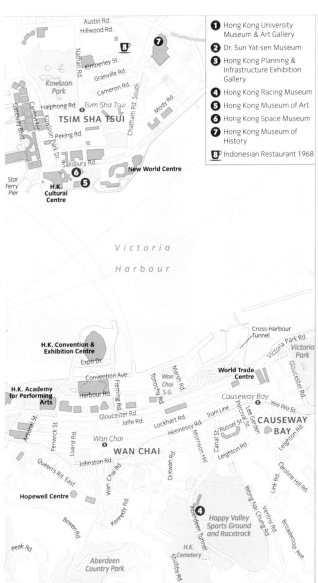

1 Hong Kong University Museum & Art Gallery
2 Dr. Sun Yat-sen Museum
3 Hong Kong Planning & Infrastructure Exhibition Gallery
4 Hong Kong Racing Museum
5 Hong Kong Museum of Art
6 Hong Kong Space Museum
7 Hong Kong Museum of History
8 Indonesian Restaurant 1968

If you're looking for great museums full of awe-inspiring sculptures and paintings, you probably should have gone to Europe. But if you want to learn about Chinese culture and history and see some fascinating ancient and contemporary Chinese art, Hong Kong has everything you'll need. And since many of the museums and galleries, offering everything from paintings to the history of horse racing, are small, you'll be able to see a great deal in just 1 day.
START: **Bus 23, 20, or 40M from Admiralty.**

❶ ★★★ Hong Kong University Museum & Art Gallery.

Located on Hong Kong University's campus, this museum houses Chinese antiquities, including pieces dating from the Neolithic period to China's Qing dynasty. The dazzling collection of bronze works date from the Shang (1600–1040 B.C.) to the Tang dynasties (A.D. 618–907). The museum also has the largest collection of Yuan dynasty Nestorian crosses—which unfortunately look like swastikas—in the world. ⌚ *1 hr. 94 Bonham Rd. Admission free. Mon–Sat 9:30am–6pm; Sun 1:30–5:30pm. Bus: 23, 20, or 40M from Admiralty.*

An ancient ceramic Buddha on display at the University Museum & Art Gallery.

❷ ★★ Dr. Sun Yat-sen Museum.

Dr. Sun Yat-sen is often called the father of modern China—in 1911 he helped overthrow the Qing dynasty and end thousands of years of dynastic rule. He was the first provisional president when the Republic of China was founded in 1912, and he is admired by Chinese of all political leanings. He spent his early years in Hong Kong, and returned here often. This comprehensive museum details his life and his revolutionary struggles. ⌚ *1 hr. 7 Castle Rd. Free admission on Wed; $HK10 other days. Wed–Mon 10am–6pm. MTR: Central, exit D2.*

A bronze statue of Dr. Sun Yat-sen stands outside the museum that bears his name.

❸ ★★ Hong Kong Planning & Infrastructure Exhibition Gallery.

This gallery traces the development of the city and shows what's in store for the future (such as the plans for new construction and development on Central's waterfront). There's also a 185m-long (607-ft.) 3-D model of the city. ⌚ *30 min. G/F 3 Edinburgh Place. Free admission. Wed–Mon 10am–6pm. MTR: Central, exit K.*

❹ ★★ Hong Kong Racing Museum.

Tracing Hong Kong's racing scene from its beginnings in the 1840s to today, this museum looks at the trainers and jockeys who made the industry a success. You'll find memorabilia, wax figures of jockeys, and a movie theater with footage of Happy Valley's past. ⌚ *45 min. Free admission. Tues–Sun 10am–5pm. 2/F*

Happy Valley Stand. MTR: Causeway Bay, exit A. Bus: 75, 90, or 97 from Exchange Square.

⑤ ★★★ Hong Kong Museum of Art.

This museum has hundreds of oil paintings, drawings, and etchings, as well as lithographs of historic Hong Kong that illustrate the city's past. But perhaps most interesting are the works of modern Hong Kong artists, such as the ink paintings of Chou Lu-gun and the oil paintings of Wang Hai, many of which fuse China's artistic tradition of calligraphy and landscapes with modern themes. ⏱ *1 hr. 10 Salisbury Rd. $HK10 adults; $HK5 children, students and seniors. Sun–Wed & Fri 10am–6pm; Sat 10am–8pm. MTR: Tsim Sha Tsui, exit E. See p 29, bullet ⑤.*

⑥ kids Hong Kong Space Museum.

With engaging, hands-on exhibits, the space museum is fun for kids and adults alike. My personal favorite is the Hall of Astronomy, which presents information on the solar system, solar science, the stars, and the universe. Some of the exhibits are a bit dated, but the harness that let's you get a sense of what walking on the moon feels like is pretty cool. ⏱ *1 hr. 10 Salisbury Rd. Free on Wed. Exhibition halls $HK10; adults; $HK5 children,*

The planetarium at the Hong Kong Space Museum features a Zeiss star projector that can project about 9,000 stars.

A model of a Chinese junk is just one of the exhibits on display at the Hong Kong Museum of History.

students and seniors. Space Theatre $HK24–$HK32 adults; $HK12–$HK16 children, students and seniors. Mon–Wed & Fri 1–9pm; Sat–Sun 10am–9pm. MTR: Tsim Sha Tsui, exit E.

⑦ ★★★ Hong Kong Museum of History.

The ultimate primer for anyone visiting the city. Don't miss the exhibit tracing Hong Kong's history over the last 400 million years, starting with its natural history and ending with the 1997 hand over to China. There are also rotating, special exhibitions. ⏱ *1 hr. 100 Chatham Rd., S. $HK10 adults; $HK5 children and seniors. Wed–Mon 10am–6pm. Bus: 5 or 8A.*

⑧ ★★ Indonesian Restaurant 1968.

For a change of pace from Cantonese or Western food try this eatery, which serves some of the best Indonesian food in town in a comfortable, clean setting. The place is simple—there's not much atmosphere—but the service is warm and friendly. A typical Indonesian dish called *gado gado* (salad with peanut sauce), is very tasty, as is the *rendang* (spicy beef). *2–4A Observatory Court.* ☎ *852/2619-1926. $$*

Hong Kong Architecture

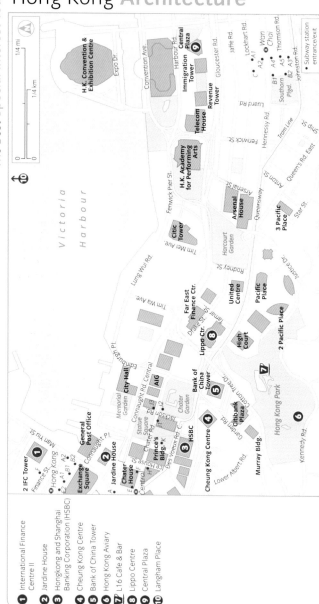

1 International Finance Centre II
2 Jardine House
3 Hongkong and Shanghai Banking Corporation (HSBC)
4 Cheung Kong Centre
5 Bank of China Tower
6 Hong Kong Aviary
7 L16 Cafe & Bar
8 Lippo Centre
9 Central Plaza
10 Langham Place

Despite Hong Kong's abundance of natural beauty, its buildings are easily its most striking feature. With millions of people living on limited land, even a run-down apartment block can be awe inspiring in its sheer size, scale, and the amount of laundry hanging from its windows. And with buildings by world-renowned architects like Cesar Pelli and Sir Norman Foster standing side by side, there's more than a bit of great architecture. Here is a look at some of Hong Kong's can't-miss construction. START: **MTR to IFC II in Central.**

❶ ★★★ International Finance Centre II. Why not begin with the tallest building in Hong Kong? The International Finance Centre II (IFC) is 415m (1,362 ft.) tall, and was completed in 2003. If you think it sticks out like a sore thumb, you're not alone—many locals complained when it first went up. The building is 88 stories high, but you won't be able to go to the top. You can, however, get up to the 55th floor, home of the Hong Kong Monetary Authority Information Centre, which is open to the public. The center has facts and exhibits about Hong

The IFC tower is one of the newer additions to Hong Kong's ever-changing skyline.

Nautical-style windows dot the exterior of Jardine House.

Kong's financial history and, of course, excellent views of the skyline. ⏱ *1 hr. 8 Finance St. Mon–Fri 10am–6pm; Sat 10am–1pm. MTR: Hong Kong, exit F.*

❷ ★★★ Jardine House. Back when it opened in 1973, this 52-story building was a symbol of how innovative and fast paced Hong Kong had become. At the time, both its size and its unique architecture—its windows look like the portholes of a ship—stood out. Today it feels a bit hidden among the massive structures in Central, but it still reflects the early days of Hong Kong's architectural boom. *1 Connaught Place. MTR: Central, exit A.*

❸ ★★★ Hongkong and Shanghai Banking Corporation (HSBC). This is one of Hong Kong's most impressive buildings, thanks to a design plan by noted British architect Sir Norman Foster. The first thing you'll notice about

the bank is its ladderlike exterior. That's because the initial plan was to build around the bank's original headquarters. The idea was scratched, but the concept of leaving a massive space in the interior of the building, running all the way up to the top floors, was maintained. In another ingenious step, Foster rejected a grand entrance hall and left the ground floor open to pedestrian traffic. ⌐ *30 min. 1 Queen's Rd. MTR: Central, exit K.*

A lion guards the entrance to the HSBC building.

❹ ★★ Cheung Kong Centre.

This 62-story building is home to many of Hong Kong's banking firms, as well as the offices of Li Ka-shing, China's richest man. Like most Hong Kong buildings, it was designed with feng shui principals in mind—the walls are black so as to absorb the negative energy of its much

A detail of the Lippo Centre's unique glass facade.

criticized neighbor, the Bank of China (see "Bank of China Tower," below). You can go inside to marvel at the 20m high (66-ft.) lobby (which is below street level, so the building's riches won't flow out), and walk to the back, where there is a garden with benches. ⌐ *30 min. 2 Queen's Rd. MTR: Central, exit J2.*

❺ ★★ Bank of China Tower.

When designing this 70-story building, Chinese-American architect I. M. Pei looked to bamboo for inspiration. He created what's essentially a flexible, though sturdy, tube. The tower has no internal structural columns, and its weight is supported by its four corner and diagonal braces. For all its structural beauty, the building has been criticized for its sharp corners. According to feng shui, those sharp corners cast negative energy on the nearby Government House and Legislative Council Building. You can visit the 43rd floor to see the view. ⌐ *30 min. 1 Garden Rd. Mon–Fri 8am–8pm; Sat–Sun 8am–2pm. MTR: Central, exit J2.*

❻ ★★★ Hong Kong Aviary.

This aviary in Hong Kong Park—a wavy structure that's home to 800 birds—was designed by a computer program. The aviary had to accommodate not only the park's undulating natural landscape, but the many trees of varying heights that would have to remain within. Designers used a

Take the escalator in Central Plaza's lobby to the elevator to the observation deck for excellent views of Hong Kong.

computer program to come up with a structure that could do just that. *1 hr. Hong Kong Park. MTR: Admiralty, exit C1. Bus: 12A.*

7 ★ **L16 Cafe & Bar.** The Thai and Western-style food served here is very good, but the real reason to come is the view of lush Hong Kong Park. The park is an outstanding example of Hong Kong's landscape architecture, and you can enjoy it either from L16's outdoor patio or from inside, where huge windows mean every seat has a view. The interior's combination of sleek wood and limestone give it an earthy feel, and the menu has dishes as varied as green chicken curry and Boston lobster bisque. Both are excellent. *Hong Kong Park.* ☎ 852/2522-6333. $$.

8 ★★★ **Lippo Centre.** It may not be the prettiest building in Hong Kong, but the Lippo Center is probably the most eye-catching. It consists of two hexagonal towers covered in reflective glass, all hovering above Admiralty's pedestrian network. The towers were designed

Langham Place is a stylish mall in the midst of an otherwise run-down neighborhood.

The Bank of China building rises dramatically over the colonial-era Legislative Council Building.

by American architect Paul Rudolph and the construction was finished in 1987. *10 min. 89 Queensway. MTR: Admiralty, exit B.*

9 ★★ **Central Plaza.** The second tallest building in Hong Kong feels a little dated with its gold and silver motif. But not so long ago (in the 1990s), Central Plaza was the tallest building in Asia at 342m (1,122 ft.). That title is long gone, but the building still offers a fantastic view of the skyline. Head for the observation floor, and take a moment to relax and enjoy the quiet as you check out the teeming city below. There's no place to sit, but there are also no crowds. *45 min. 18 Harbour Rd. MTR: Wan Chai, exit A5.*

10 ★★ **Langham Place.** Malls are not my favorite places to spend time, but even I enjoy riding the long escalator at the center of Langham Place, a gargantuan high-end shopping center. The escalator rises up through a series of floors filled with shops and restaurants, while offering superb views of the gritty streets of Mongkok through its huge windows. *1 hr. 555 Shanghai St. MTR: Mongkok, exit C3.*

British Hong Kong

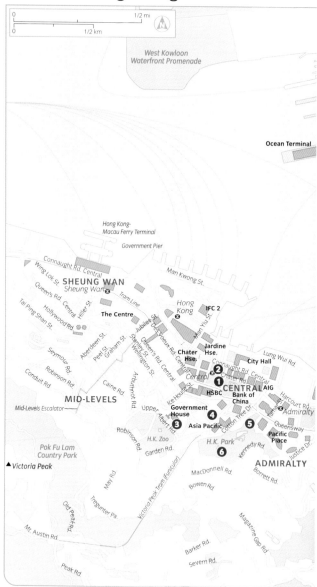

West Kowloon
Waterfront Promenade

Ocean Terminal

Hong Kong-
Macau Ferry Terminal

Government Pier

Connaught Rd. Central

Man Kwong St.

Wing Lok St.
Queen's Rd. Central
SHEUNG WAN
Sheung Wan

Tram Line

Hiller St.

Hong Kong

IFC 2

Tai Ping Shan St.
Hollywood Rd.

The Centre

Jubilee St.

Man Yiu St.

Aberdeen St.

Peel St.

Graham St.

Stanley St.

Des Voeux Rd. Central

Queen's Rd. Central

Wellington St.

**Jardine
Hse.**

Lung Wui Rd.

Seymour Rd.

**Chater
Hse.**

City Hall

Central

Connaught Rd. Central

Robinson Rd.

Caine Rd.

Arbuthnot Rd.

Upper

Ice House St.

Chater Rd.

❷
❶

HSBC

**Bank of
China**

AIG

Harcourt Rd.

Conduit Rd.

MID-LEVELS

Mid-Levels Escalator

**Government
House**

❹

Admiralty

Queensway

Cotton Tree Dr.

❺

**Pacific
Place**

Robinson Rd.

Albert Rd.

❸

Asia Pacific

Justice Dr.

H.K. Zoo

Garden Rd.

H.K. Park

❻

Kennedy Rd.

ADMIRALTY

Pok Fu Lam
Country Park

May Rd.

Tregunter Pa.

Victoria Peak Tram (Funicular)

MacDonnell Rd.

Borrett Rd.

▲Victoria Peak

Bowen Rd.

Magazine Gap Rd.

Mt. Austin Rd.

Old Peak Rd.

Barker Rd.

Severn Rd.

Peak Rd.

0 — 1/2 mi
0 — 1/2 km

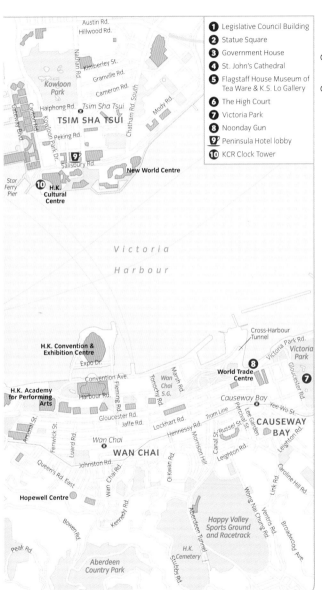

1 Legislative Council Building
2 Statue Square
3 Government House
4 St. John's Cathedral
5 Flagstaff House Museum of Tea Ware & K.S. Lo Gallery
6 The High Court
7 Victoria Park
8 Noonday Gun
9 Peninsula Hotel lobby
10 KCR Clock Tower

The British, who were looking for new trading ports in the Far East, captured Hong Kong in 1842, when it was still a quiet Chinese fishing village with only 7,000 residents. The Brits nabbed Kowloon in 1860 and arranged a lease for the New Territories in 1898. But under a treaty with China, Great Britain was obligated to hand it all back in 1997. And while Hong Kong retained its Chinese heritage, even as a rapidly growing colony, more than a hint of British influence remains. The harbor is named for Queen Victoria; colonial buildings dot the city; and Britishisms like "spot of tea" pepper the local English. So don't be surprised if you sometimes feel you're closer to London than Beijing. START: **MTR to Statue Square in Central.**

❶ ★★ Legislative Council Building. Built in 1812, this was formerly the Supreme Court (hence the Greek god of justice, Themis, looking down from above). Now it's where the Hong Kong equivalent of Congress, known as Legco, meets. Delegates are elected, but there's also a "functional constituency" branch run by pro-Beijing business factions which help ensure the government stays loyal to China. The chief executive, Hong Kong's equivalent of a president, is also chosen by Beijing. Call ahead to reserve seats if you want to see this pseudodemocracy in action. *30 min. 8 Jackson Rd.* ☎ *852/2869-9399. MTR: Central, exit J1.*

❷ ★ Statue Square. This square was built toward the end of the

The Greek god of justice stands atop the Legislative Council Building.

What would the queen think? A replica of a Buckingham Palace guard's uniform for sale on Cat St in Hong Kong.

1800s and was so named because it originally contained a statue of Queen Victoria. The Japanese pulled the statue out when they invaded during World War II and it now stands in Victoria Park. Today, the square is home to a memorial to those who died in the two world wars. There's also a statue of Sir Thomas Jackson, a manager of the Hongkong and Shanghai Banking Corporation (HSBC) in the 1870s, which is fitting as you can see the HSBC building in the distance. *15 min. Chater Rd. and Des Voeux Rd. MTR: Central, exit K.*

❸ ★ Government House. Built in 1855, this white stucco house was home to most of Hong Kong's British governors. During World War II it was the headquarters for the Japanese commander, who added the Shinto shrine–style tower and the ceramic roof tiles. When the first Chinese leader, Tung Chee-hwa, came to power in 1997 he lived elsewhere because the building had bad feng shui (or just bad political history). The current chief executive, Donald Tsang, doesn't seem to mind. ⏱ *30 min. Upper Albert Rd. www.ceo.gov.hk. Bus: 3B, 12, 23, or 103.*

The Shinto shrine–style tower at the British-built Government House.

❹ ★ St. John's Cathedral. Founded in 1849 by Christian missionaries, the oldest Anglican church in Hong Kong is shaped like a cross, with a large, airy interior and beautiful stained-glass windows. Here in Hong Kong, with the city's skyscrapers looming in the background, a visit to the church makes for a stark contrast not only between the past and present, but also between the idealism of the missionaries and the realities of capitalism. ⏱ *30 min. 4–8 Garden Rd. www.stjohnscathedral.org.hk. Daily 6am–7pm. MTR: Central, exit J2. See p 49, bullet ❶.*

❺ ★★ Flagstaff House Museum of Tea Ware and K.S. Lo Gallery. This Greek revival–style home was built in 1846 and is the oldest colonial building in Hong Kong. It's a prime example of colonial architecture and was originally the home of the commander of the British forces. Fittingly, it's now a tea museum showcasing tea ware from many Chinese dynasties. The attached K.S. Lo Gallery also has a variety of antique Chinese ceramics and Chinese seals. ⏱ *1 hr. Hong Kong Park. 10 Cotton Tree Dr. Wed–Mon 10am–5pm. Free admission. MTR: Admiralty, exit C1.*

❻ ★★ The High Court. This rather bland-looking high-rise was made the home of Hong Kong's Supreme Court after the 1997 hand over to China. But in typical British fashion, the barristers here wear white wigs while arguing cases

St. John's Cathedral now sits in the shadow of skyscrapers.

At the High Court, lawyers and judges still wear wigs, in typical British style.

(which can be heard in Chinese, English, or both). Stop by for a very visual reminder of Britain's rule. *30 min. Time varies depending on cases. 38 Queensway Rd. MTR: Central, exit J2.*

⑦ ★★ Victoria Park. Look for the statue of Queen Victoria (it's the one that used to be in Statue Square). It was restored and placed here in 1952. This shady park has tennis courts, soccer fields, and many quiet (and cool) spots to take a break. *30 min. MTR: Causeway Bay, exit E; Tin Hau, exit A2.*

⑧ ★ Noonday Gun. This cannon, a loud reminder of Hong Kong's British past, was built in 1901 and is fired every day at 12pm in a longstanding British tradition. It's across the street from the Excelsior Hotel. *20 min. 221 Gloucester Rd. MTR: Causeway Bay, exit D1.*

⑨ ★★★ Peninsula Hotel Lobby. This hotel was built in 1928

and quickly became a stopover point for the wealthiest and most famous business people, diplomats, and travelers visiting Asia. The squat building in front is original—the tower you see behind it was added in 1994. Thanks to the number of British guests who passed through, the Peninsula's ornate lobby has long been a popular place to come for afternoon tea—a live band plays relaxing music from a balcony above the crowd. *Salisbury Rd. ☎ 852/2920-2888. See p 17, bullet ⑧.*

⑩ ★★ KCR Clock Tower. The KCR Clock Tower is a British icon that today seems sadly out of place. Flanked by a Starbucks and a bus stop, the tower, completed in 1910, once marked the terminus of the Kowloon-Canton Railway (KCR). At that time, the KCR was one of the main modes of transportation into Hong Kong. But the city decided that land this close to the water should be put to better use and it moved the train station to make way for a promenade, shops, and museums, leaving only this tower behind as a reminder. *10 min. Star Ferry terminal. MTR: Tsim Sha Tsui, exit E. Star Ferry.* ●

Afternoon tea at the Peninsula Hotel is an elegant Hong Kong tradition.

Yau Ma Tei & Mongkok

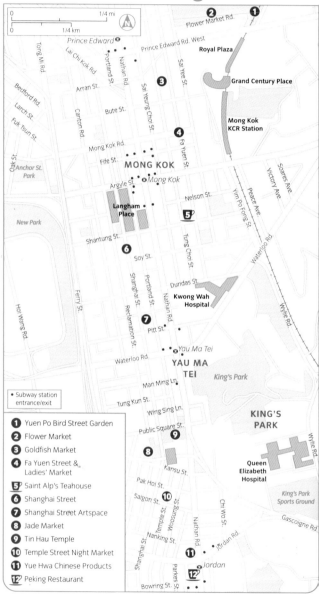

• Subway station entrance/exit

Previous page: Bamboo bird cages for sale at the Bird Market.

This walk will take you into Kowloon's Yau Ma Tei and Mongkok neighborhoods. It's the heart of residential Hong Kong, where hoards of locals hustle past on their daily rounds. If you can handle the crowds, you'll be rewarded with a true taste of the city's daily life. You'll mix with all kinds of people as you explore these streets, from teenage boys with spiked haircuts to elderly women in traditional Chinese silks. START: **B1 exit of the Prince Edward MTR station, walk east along Prince Edward Road West.**

❶ ★★ Yuen Po Street Bird Garden. You'll enter this market through a "pai lou," or gateway, to find a series of courtyards with more than 70 stalls selling birds like cockatoos and parakeets, along with cages, seed, and even fresh grasshoppers (apparently a bird delicacy). Keep an eye out for locals who have brought their beloved pet birds here for a day on the town and a little socializing (both for the owners and their feathered friends). 30 min.

❷ ★ Flower Market. This teeming market is easily one of the most aromatic spots in Hong Kong. It also has a compelling collection of bonsai. Treat yourself to a bouquet of roses or other choice blossoms. 30 min.

❸ Goldfish Market. The Chinese believe fish bring good luck,

Birds, like this one for sale at the Bird Market, are prized pets here; prices are based on singing ability, not plumage.

You can buy orchids, and other blooms, at the Flower Market.

and that aquariums add great feng shui to any room. This narrow street is packed, well, to the gills, with shops carrying everything from goldfish to more exotic tropical varieties. They're on display in tanks and in water-filled baggies that hang from doorways. Pet lovers, beware: Most of the fish are kept in overcrowded tanks, and you'll also see puppies, kittens, and turtles waiting for homes in some of the cramped shops. 30 min.

❹ ★★ Fa Yuen Street and the Ladies' Market. Fa Yuen Street is a local market made up of small shops selling clothing, handbags, toys, and loads of other goods at cheap prices. A little digging may be required to find what you want. The nearby Ladies' Market (see p 13, bullet ❼), a long street of canopied

Bags of goldfish hang in a doorway at the Goldfish Market. See p 41.

stalls, is a bit more organized. There's a huge selection, ranging from jeans and silk dresses to pens and watches. But watch out for the counterfeit goods—they're cheap for a reason (namely, they usually don't last very long). 1 hr.

5 **Saint Alp's Teahouse.** This popular teahouse, which is part of a chain that has spread to the U.S., is a trendy spot to take a break while shopping. You can cool off with an Indian mango tea or frothy tea with pearl tapioca, and munch on crispy chicken, vegetables, and rice, or Taiwanese-style marinated minced pork with steamed rice. *61A Shantung St.* ☎ *852/2782-1438. $.*

6 **Shanghai Street.** Chinese couples come here for traditional wedding outfits, which are usually red and stitched with elaborate gold and silver designs like phoenixes and dragons. While the trade has slowed a bit in recent years, these shops offer a fascinating glimpse of Hong Kong's Chinese heritage. 20 min.

7 ★★ **Shanghai Street Artspace.** Much of the work shown here is cutting edge for Hong Kong—computer art, multimedia exhibits, and video works by local artists and designers. Funded by the Hong Kong Arts Development Council, it's a sign of the increased attention the city is paying to its creative sphere. 30 min. 404 Shanghai St. Tues–Sun 11am–2pm and 3–8pm.

8 **Jade Market.** True to its name, this market consists of about 400 dealers selling jade—everything from small pendants to large sculptures. A word of warning: judging the quality of jade can be tricky. Think twice before spending large sums here, as foreigners are sometimes taken for a ride. If you like a piece but aren't sure the price is fair, ask if they'll allow you to have it tested for authenticity at the nearby Jade Plaza on Jade Road (between Canton Rd. and Kansu St.). 30 min.

9 ★★ **Tin Hau Temple.** Burning incense hangs from the high ceilings at this Buddhist temple, sections of which date back over 100 years. Tin

Inexpensive jade jewelry is for sale at the Jade Market.

The Tin Hau Temple is one of the oldest Buddhist temples in Hong Kong.

Hau is dedicated to the goddess of seafarers—it may seem hard to believe now, but the temple was once on the waterfront. Massive reclamation has left it very much inland. ⏱ *30 min. Daily 8am–5pm.*

⑩ ★★★ Temple Street Night Market. This market, which starts setting up around 4pm and stays open until midnight, has a very big draw: the dai pai dong stands selling delicious fried noodles and seafood. Sure, you can browse the DVDs, clothing, and other items, but I recommend grabbing a stool at one of the outdoor tables and enjoying the scene. You'll find fortunetellers, musicians, and the occasional Cantonese opera singer belting out a song at the market's northern end (see p 13, bullet **⑧**). ⏱ *1hr. Daily 4pm–midnight.*

⑪ ★ Yue Hwa Chinese Products. This huge emporium sells uniquely Chinese goods brought in from the mainland. Its seven floors house ceramics, silks, and herbs—pretty much anything and everything you might hope to buy while in Hong Kong. Of the several branches of this store, this one is the best, and it's open until 10pm. ⏱ *1 hr. 301–309 Nathan Rd.* ☎ *852/3511-2222. www.yuehwa.com. Daily 10am–10pm.*

⑫ Peking Restaurant. While the best Peking duck is, of course, found in Beijing, this is one of my favorite spots for the dish in Hong Kong. The restaurant's interior is nondescript, but the food isn't—the skin of the duck is crispy and the meat is juicy. The dish is served in the traditional manner, with thin pancakes, green Chinese onions, and a sweet, thick sauce. Other northern Chinese dishes, such as kung pao chicken and mapo doufu (spicy tofu with ground pork), are also on offer here. *227 Nathan Rd.* ☎ *852/2730-1315. $$.*

A Taste of the Past

Dai pai dong, (which literally means "big rows of food stalls,") is a dying tradition in Hong Kong. These outdoor eateries, known for their cheap, good food, were all over the city less than 50 years ago. But hygiene concerns, increased wealth, and changes in eating habits have led the government to move most of these stalls into covered markets. The dai pai dong at Temple Street and in Central near SoHo are among the few remaining to have maintained their original feel. While they don't usually have English menus, the waiters are generally quite helpful.

The Best Walk in **Tsim Sha Tsui**

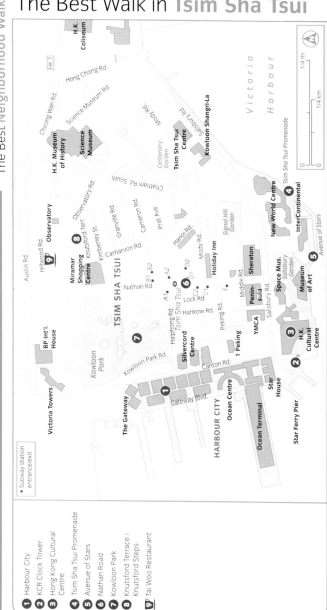

1 Harbour City
2 KCR Clock Tower
3 Hong Kong Cultural Centre
4 Tsim Sha Tsui Promenade
5 Avenue of Stars
6 Nathan Road
7 Kowloon Park
8 Knutsford Terrace / Knutsford Steps
9 Tai Woo Restaurant

• Subway station entrance/exit

HARBOUR CITY

Ocean Terminal

Ocean Centre

Star House

Star Ferry Pier

The Gateway

Gateway Blvd.

Silvercord Centre

Canton Rd.

Kowloon Park Rd.

Kowloon Park

Haiphong Rd.

Hankow Rd.

Peking Rd.

1 Peking

Lock Rd.

Nathan Rd.

A1 A2 B1 B2 C1 C2 D1 D2 E

YMCA

Peninsula

Sheraton

Salisbury Rd.

Middle Rd.

Space Mus.
Salisbury Garden

Museum of Art

H.K. Cultural Centre

Signal Hill Garden

New World Centre

InterContinental

Avenue of Stars

Tsim Sha Tsui Promenade

Kowloon Shangri-La

Tsim Sha Tsui Centre

Centenary Garden

Chatham Rd. South

Prat Ave.

Cameron Rd.

Granville Rd.

Kimberley St.

Knutsford Terr.

Carnarvon Rd.

Hanoi Rd.

Moby Rd.

Holiday Inn

Mody Rd.

Salisbury Rd.

TSIM SHA TSUI

Tsim Sha Tsui

Miramar Shopping Centre

Observatory

Observatory Rd.

Hillwood Rd.

Austin Rd.

BP Int'l. House

Victoria Towers

Kowloon Park Rd.

Cheong Wan Rd.

Hong Chong Rd.

HK 1

Science Museum Rd.

H.K. Museum of History

Science Museum

H.K. Coliseum

Victoria Harbour

0 1/4 mi
0 1/4 km

N

This walk will take you from Hong Kong's Avenue of Stars through the Golden Mile, the city's (much smaller) version of New York City's Fifth Avenue. With restaurants, cinemas, and yes, of course, countless shops, Tsim Sha Tsui (TST) is the heart of entertainment and tourism in Hong Kong. Its crowded streets will exhilarate and leave you happily exhausted. START: the Star Ferry terminal in Tsim Sha Tsui.

1 **kids** **Harbour City.** Housing more than 600 high-end and midrange shops, 4 hotels, some 50 restaurants, and 2 cinemas, this mall is one of the largest in Asia. It also has stunning views of the harbor, in addition to its designer goods (including Louis Vuitton, Ferragamo, and Prada) and jade jewelry boutiques. If you're traveling with children (and ready to shop), don't miss the KidX section, which includes the largest Toys "R" Us in Asia. *1 hr. 3–27 Canton Rd.* ☎ *852/2118-8601. www.harbourcity.com.hk. Daily 10am–9pm; some shops closed on Sunday.*

2 ★ **KCR Clock Tower.** This spot used to be the terminus of the Kowloon-Canton Railway—the end point for those who crossed Europe

The Kowloon-Canton Railway Clock Tower is a symbol of Hong Kong's rapidly fading colonial past.

Enjoy a quiet stroll along the Tsim Sha Tsui Promenade. See p 46.

and much of Asia by train to get here. Today, all that's left is the red-brick and concrete clock tower, built by the British government in 1915. But the Kowloon-Canton Railway terminus moved to Hung Hom in 1975, and the clock became a symbol of Hong Kong's British past. *Star Ferry terminal, Tsim Sha Tsui. See p 38, bullet* **10**.

3 ★★ **Hong Kong Cultural Centre.** Opened in 1989 on the site of the former Kowloon-Canton Railway station, this saddle-shaped monstrosity (a waterfront building with no windows?) is Hong Kong's largest center for performing arts. Stop by to pick up tickets. There are free family performances, ranging from traditional Chinese dance to magic shows, on Saturdays from 2.30 to 4:30pm. *30 min. 10 Salisbury*

The British Are Coming

Although Hong Kong is clearly a Chinese city, it was actually under British rule from 1842 to 1997, when Great Britain handed the reins back to China. In the early part of the 19th century, Britain was desperate for Chinese tea and silks, but China wasn't interested in trade—that is, until the British introduced opium they imported from India. Addiction ran rampant at every level of Chinese society, and the emperor banned opium imports in the 1830s. British traders ignored the ban, leading to the start of the First Opium War in 1839. When the war ended in 1842, China handed over Hong Kong as part of the settlement. The Second Opium War (1856–1858) resulted in the loss of Kowloon.

Rd. ☎ 852/2734-9009. *www. hkculturalcentre.gov.hk.* Box office open daily 10am–9:30pm.

④ ★★★ Tsim Sha Tsui Promenade. From this waterfront promenade you'll get one of the most impressive views of the skyline in all of Hong Kong. And you'll be reminded of the city's seafaring past (which can be surprisingly easy to forget, given the urban feel) as everything from the Star Ferries to private junks, cruise ships, and mas-

Massive neon signs dominate Hong Kong's high-end shopping street Nathan Road.

sive cargo boats glide past. 🕐 *30 min. Star Ferry terminal, Tsim Sha Tsui.*

⑤ Avenue of Stars. It's a bit kitschy, but Avenue of Stars is also a lot of fun. You'll find plaques (complete with handprints) in honor of some of Hong Kong's most famous films stars here. See if your hand is bigger than Jackie Chan's. 🕐 *20 min. Tsim Sha Tsui promenade. Tsim Sha Tsui. See p 13, bullet* **⑨**.

⑥ ★ Nathan Road. Kowloon's most famous shopping street runs up the peninsula to Boundary Road, the official spot where the New Territories begins. The noisy bustle and neon signs are charming even if you're not in the market for high-end jewelry, clothing, and electronics. Watch for the Lacoste boutique, right near its local competitor, Crocodile. 🕐 *1 hr. See p 12, bullet* **④**.

⑦ ★ Kowloon Park. Kowloon Park is one of the city's most diverse and peaceful, and it offers a variety of gardens, including a water garden, a Chinese garden, and a sculpture garden. There's also a large aviary, a walking trail enveloped by trees, and public swimming pools. If you're here on a Sunday from 2:30

to 4:30pm, you may see people performing martial arts. The park is also home to the Hong Kong Heritage Discovery Centre, which has an exhibition gallery and library that are open to the public. Frankly, the Centre doesn't have too much of interest, but you can duck inside to enjoy the air-conditioning if the weather is hot. ⏱ *30 min.*

The sculpture garden is just one of Kowloon Park's many charms.

❽ ★★ Knutsford Terrace/ Knutsford Steps. This row of bars and restaurants is located at the top of a set of stairs on a car-free street, and caters to tourists and expatriates. The scene tends to be young and lively, with diners and drinkers mingling at tables lining the terrace. There are darts and other games in some of the bars, as well as televisions for sports events. If you're ready for a break, try Bahama Mama's (see p 96), which has a laid-back atmosphere and a huge beer selection. ⏱ *20 min.*

❾ ☕ ★ Tai Woo Restaurant. Cantonese cuisine is a Hong Kong specialty, and this is a great place to try it. Sure, the menu offers local favorites like scrambled egg whites with crab meat served with prawns in salted egg yolk and breaded and deep-fried oysters. But perhaps more importantly, it has the raucous, banquet-style atmosphere that's typical of traditional Cantonese restaurants. Though part of a chain, this branch is by far the best. *14–16 Hillwood Rd.* ☎ *852/ 2368-5420.* *$$.*

Celluloid City

Thanks to Hong Kong's political, economic, and artistic freedoms, it was the center of Chinese-language filmmaking from the 1950s into the 1990s. Although rampant piracy, a strong push into Asia by Hollywood, and stronger offerings from the rest of Asia have all cut into Hong Kong's dominance, local filmmakers such as Wong Kar-wai and Stephen Chow continue to make internationally popular Cantonese-language films. Perhaps more dominant, however, is the influence of Hong Kong's kung fu and action movies on the world of film. This is epitomized by that legendary man of action, Jackie Chan, whose star is on the Avenue of Stars as well as the Hollywood Walk of Fame. Two of my favorite Hong Kong movies—and the perfect DVDs to keep you entertained on your long flight—are Wong's violent but touching *Fallen Angels* and Chow's hilarious *Kung Fu Hustle*.

The Best Walk in **Central** & Western

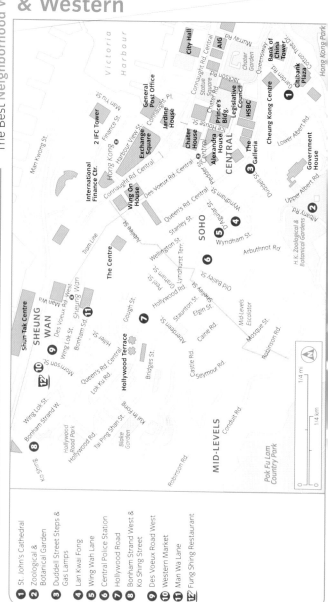

A good walk in Hong Kong is almost always going to involve shopping and eating. But a walk through these neighborhoods also gives you a chance to see life on the streets, where vegetable vendors chat on expensive cellphones and financial consultants cram into small booths to slurp noodles and drink tea. You'll head through lush Hong Kong Park, pass beneath towering skyscrapers, and eventually end up in the midst of a Chinese residential area.
START: **Hong Kong Park.**

❶ ★ St. John's Cathedral.
This breathtaking, Gothic-style church is worth visiting not only for its stained-glass windows and its uniquely tropical touches (like ceiling fans), but also for its historic significance. Built by missionaries in 1847, it is believed to be the oldest Anglican church in the Far East. During World War II, it was a social club for the occupying Japanese forces. Today, Hong Kong's large Filipino population uses it as a religious base, and services are given in English, Mandarin, and Tagalog. 🕐 *30 min. 4–8 Garden Rd. Daily 7am–6pm. See p 37, bullet* ❹.

❷ ★★ kids Zoological & Botanical Garden.
Founded in 1864, this garden maintains much of its Victorian charm, despite the skyscrapers in the distance. There's a wrought-iron greenhouse, a terrace garden, and a playground with slides and swings. Farther into the

The Duddell Street gas lamps are a charming reminder of Hong Kong's colonial past.

park, you'll find the animals, including panda bears. An aviary is home to some 160 types of birds, including red-crown cranes, flamingos, and peacock pheasants. 🕐 *45 min. Albany Rd.* 📞 *852/2530-0154. Daily 6am–7pm.*

❸ Duddell Street Steps & Gas Lamps.
The wide stone steps that connect Duddell Street and Ice House Street are a reminder of a time before the Mid-Levels escalator whisked people up and down the lower parts of Victoria Peak. In this city of neon, the beautiful old gas lamps—installed between 1875 and 1889 and the last remaining in the city—lining the steps are particularly

A panda enjoys a bamboo snack at the Zoological & Botanical Garden.

What's an SAR?

You may hear Hong Kong referred to as an SAR, which stands for Special Administrative Region. That's because when the British handed the city back to Communist China in 1997, they negotiated an arrangement that allowed citizens of Hong Kong to retain certain rights for 50 years. The end result is that Hong Kong has far more economic and cultural freedoms than most of China. It's ostensibly run by a freely elected government, though many would say that Beijing really calls the shots, since the Chinese government plays a major role in choosing officials.

evocative of days past. ⏱ *20 min. Duddell St.*

4 ★ **Lan Kwai Fong.** Though this district is best known for its nightlife, walking through Lan Kwai Fong in the daytime will give you a more relaxed (and possibly more clear-eyed) look at an area that has become a part of Hong Kong's cultural identity. It's packed full of bars, restaurants, and shops, some of them on the second and third floors. Enjoy the quiet—if you come back in the evening, as you surely

The Central Police Station is one of the best remaining examples of classical-style architecture in Hong Kong.

will, you'll hardly recognize the place. ⏱ *30 min. Lan Kwai Fong. See p 18, bullet* **9**.

5 **Wing Wah Lane.** Wing Wah Lane, also known as "Rat Alley" thanks to its narrowness, is home to a collection of restaurants serving Malaysian, Thai, and Indian food, as well as American hamburgers. The atmosphere is laid-back and festive, with folding tables out in the street under canopies. Of all of the options here, I suggest **Good Luck Thai** for its outstanding pad thai, tom yum soups, and cold Singha beer.

6 **Central Police Station.** You can't miss this collection of massive gray buildings—it's the largest cluster of Victorian architecture left in the city. Part of the compound, once both police headquarters and a prison, dates back to 1864 (the rest was built in 1910 and 1925). Now, it's a relic of the past with an uncertain future. Some have called for it to be torn down to make way for new construction. But in a move that gives hope to the city's preservationists, it looks more likely that the government will renovate it into restaurants, a museum, and art galleries. *10 Hollywood Rd.*

7 ★★ **Hollywood Road.** This road was built in 1844 by the British army and was named after the holly

Hollywood Road is one of the best places to shop for antiques and for uniquely Chinese souvenirs like this wooden Buddha mask.

shrubs that lined it. Check out the many antiques shops that line the road and you'll find a fascinating range of Chinese sculpture, calligraphy, and furniture. If your feet are tired from all this walking, stop in for a quick foot massage at Central Salon and Spa. 🕐 *1 hr. See p 7, bullet* ❹.

❽ ★★ Bonham Strand West (Ginseng and Bird's Nest sts.) and Ko Shing Street (Herbal Medicine St.). Possession Street, also known as Shui Hang Hau, is where the British first landed when they came to Hong Kong in 1841. As you can see (or not see, as there's no water nearby), the harbor has been filled in significantly since then in a

process known as reclamation. It's now part of an area, bounded by the streets listed above, famous for its very old, very Chinese goods. Shops along this street sell ginseng and bird's nest used for both cooking and medicine (see "Chinese Medicine," below). 🕐 *1 hr.*

❾ ★ Des Voeux Road West (Dried Seafood St.). Des Voeux Road specializes in products you might not see at home—namely, dried seafood. As you stroll past towering apartment blocks, you'll see shop fronts cluttered with huge bags of dried shrimp, shark fins, oysters, and more. Perhaps not surprisingly, the smell is overwhelming. 🕐 *30 min.*

Bird's nest, for sale along Bonham Strand West, is a delicacy in Hong Kong. The nests are those of certain types of swifts.

Chinese Medicine

Though Hong Kong is thoroughly modern, many Chinese don't view Western medicine as the best the 21st century has to offer. They put more stock in traditional remedies dating back thousands of years. You'll see shops selling plant roots, fossilized bones, animal teeth, and deer's horn. Deer's horn is said to be effective against fever. Bones, teeth, and seashells are used as tranquilizers and cures for insomnia. If you have indigestion, a stuffed-up nose, a backache, or any other nagging pain (and you're not afraid to drink a mixture of crushed animal teeth), see if you can't get an herbalist to give you a remedy. You can always mime your symptoms—he'll probably figure out what you mean.

A herbal medicine dealer measures out some of his wares. See p 51.

⑩ Western Market. This red-brick building is the oldest surviving market building in the city—another positive sign in a place where old architecture often gets bulldozed. It's also an excellent (and rare) example of Edwardian architecture. The shops inside aren't terribly special, but they do sell clothing, tea, and souvenirs like Chinese seals and jade jewelry. The top floor features an afternoon ballroom dancing exhibition from

Exploring the dried seafood shops is a fascinating, albeit aromatic, experience. See p 51.

2:30 to 6pm; you can watch for free, but unless you speak Cantonese it will probably be difficult to join in the fun. 30 min. 323 Des Voeux Rd. See p 21, bullet ②.

⑪ Man Wa Lane. This street has been home to one of China's oldest trades—carved seal making—since the 1920s. The stalls look a bit out of place tucked amid high-rises, but they carry traditional seals and stamps made of jade, clay, marble, and other materials. You can have a seal, or "chop," custom-made at several of the booths here—it takes about an hour, so you may want to stop by to pick your order up after you finish this walk. 30 min.

⑫ ★★ Fung Shing Restaurant. Located right near the Western Market, this Chinese restaurant has a large menu (with plenty of pictures to help you choose), and offers classics such as shark's fin with shredded chicken or fried sliced pigeon. The waitstaff is efficient and friendly, and the portions are huge and served piping hot. *7 On Tai St.* ☎ *852/2815-8689. $$$.* ●

Shopping Best Bets

Best Chinese-Themed Gifts
★★ Chinese Arts and Crafts, *3 Salisbury Rd.* (p 61)

Best Contemporary Art
★★★ Hanart T Z Gallery, *202 Henley Building, 2/Fl, 5 Queen's Rd.* (p 59)

Best Designer Clothing
★★ Joyce Boutique, *18 Queen's Rd.* (p 62)

Best Jade Statues & Bracelets
★ Jade Market, *between Kansu and Battery sts.* (p 65)

Best Cheap Electronics
★★★ Wan Chai Computer Centre, *130 Hennessy Rd.* (p 62)

Best English-Language Books & Magazines
★★★ Swindon Book Co. Ltd., *13–15 Lock Rd.* (p 60)

Best Cheap Souvenirs
★ Cat Street, *Upper Lascar Row* (p 65)

Best Pottery
★ Dragon Culture, *231 Hollywood Rd.* (p 58)

Best Ceramics
★★ Overjoy *Kwai Hing Industrial Building, 10–18 Chun Pin St., Block B, 1st floor* (p 60)

Best Chinese Furniture
★★ China Art, *15 Hollywood Rd.* (p 58)

Best Hand-Woven Carpets
★★ Chinese Carpet Centre, *Shop 168, Ocean Terminal, Zone C, Harbour City, Canton Rd.* (p 60)

Best Night Shopping
★★★ Temple Street Night Market, *34 Temple St.* (p 65)

Best Local Fashion
★★★ G.O.D., *Leighton Centre Sharp St. East* (p 62)

Best Chinese Medicine
★★★ Eu Yan Sang, *152–156 Queen's Rd.* (p 65)

Best Mall
★★★ IFC Mall, *8 Finance St.* (p 64)

Best Antiques for All Budgets
★★★ Arch Angel Antiques, *53–55 Hollywood Rd.* (p 58)

The tailors at Sam's are world-famous for their custom-made suits and shirts. See p 66.

Kowloon Shopping

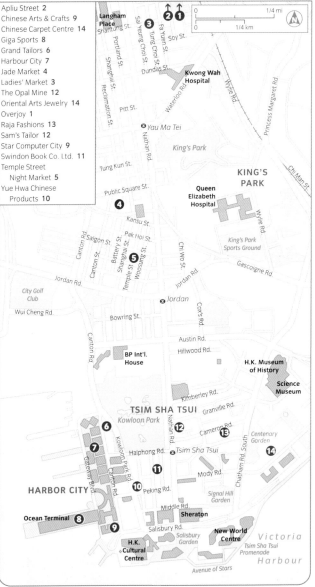

Photo p 53: Inexpensive Chinese silk dresses at the Temple Street Night Market.

Central Shopping

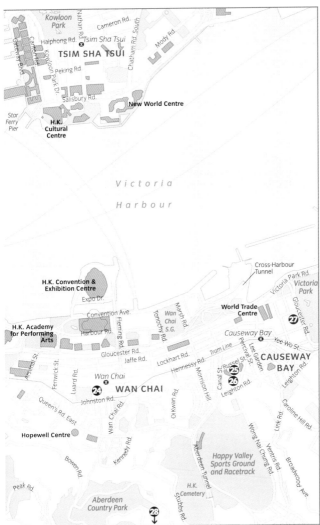

Shopping A to Z

Antiques & Collectibles

★★★ Arch Angel Antiques

CENTRAL   There are pieces here for the serious collector—Chinese porcelain and terra cotta from the Tang (A.D. 618–907) and Ming (1368–1644) dynasties. But the shop's three floors also feature smaller items, like mahjong sets and chopsticks, perfect for casual shoppers. *53–55 Hollywood Rd.* ☎ *852/2851-6848. AE, DC, MC, V. MTR: Sheung Wan. Bus: 26. Map p 56.*

★★ China Art CENTRAL   This is

the spot for Chinese lacquered furniture. Family-owned China Art restores antiques in a workshop in Panyu, China, then ships them to Hong Kong for sale. *15 Hollywood Rd.* ☎ *852/2542-0982. www.china art.com.hk. AE, DC, MC, V. MTR: Central. Bus: 26. Map p 56.*

★ Chine Gallery CENTRAL

There's a wide selection of hand-woven rugs from Tibet, Inner Mongolia, and Xinjiang here, along with Chinese furniture dating to the mid–19th century. It's worth stopping in to see the beautiful collection of chairs from Sichuan, Shanxi, and other regions of China. Brothers Zafar and Anwer Islam, who own the place, are experts in restoration. *42A Hollywood Rd.* ☎ *852/2543-0023. www.chinegallery.com. AE, MC, V. MTR: Central. Bus: 26. Map p 56.*

★★ Dragon Culture CENTRAL

Owner Victor Choi, who also has a gallery in New York and has written books on Chinese antiques, has a huge stock of Tang dynasty pottery, Ming porcelain, snuff bottles, and other curios. The staff here are helpful and patient. ☎ *852/2545-8098. www.dragon culture.com.hk. AE, MC, V. MTR: Sheung Wan. Bus: 26. Map p 56.*

★★ Honeychurch Antiques

CENTRAL   Americans Glenn and Lucille Vessa, the Asian art dealers who run this shop, can help guide you in buying furniture and collectibles not only from China, but also from other parts of Asia. They sell furniture, paintings, pottery, and porcelain ranging from fifth millennium B.C. to the early half of the 20th century. *29 Hollywood Rd.* ☎ *852/2543-2433. www.honey church.com/hongkong. AE, DC, MC, V. MTR: Central. Bus: 26. Map p 56.*

Terracotta horses are among the many unique items for sale at Dragon Culture.

Serious collectors of Asian antiques head to Honeychurch Antiques.

Art Galleries

★ Galerie Martini CENTRAL
This gallery of contemporary multi-media art often features new discoveries. Their video installations, an increasingly popular medium among artists in southern China, are especially fascinating thanks to artists who explore themes of Hong Kong's ever-changing urban landscape. *99F Wellington St.* ☎ *852/2526-9566. AE, MC, V. MTR: Central. Map p 56.*

★★ Grotto Fine Art CENTRAL
Founded in 2001, this small, avant-garde gallery shows Chinese artists, including major Hong Kong art stars like Lu Shou Kun and newcomers like painter Chow Chun-fai. The gallery's director and curator, Henry Au-yeung, is a specialist in 20th-century Chinese art history. *31C–D Wyndham St., 2nd Floor.* ☎ *852/2121-2270. www.grotto fineart.com. AE, MC, V. MTR: Central. Map p 56.*

★★★ Hanart T Z Gallery CENTRAL   Since 1983, this gallery has been influential in helping promote local artists (primarily painters and photographers) and has earned a reputation for showing the best new work China has to offer. *202 Henley Building, 5 Queen's Rd.* ☎ *852/2526-9019. www.hanart.com. AE, MC, V. MTR: Central. Map p 56.*

★★ Plum Blossoms CENTRAL
Plum Blossoms stands out for showing Chinese textiles and antique Tibetan furniture alongside contemporary paintings and sculpture. *1 Hollywood Rd.* ☎ *852/2521-2189. www.plumblossoms.com. AE, MC, V. MTR: Central. Bus: 26. Map p 56.*

★ Schoeni Art Gallery CENTRAL
This is the best place to see cutting-edge Chinese art. Schoeni represents artists like the surrealist painter Zhang Lin Hai, whose paintings incorporate Chinese landmarks and history. *21–31 Old Bailey St.* ☎ *852/ 2869-8802. www.schoeni.com.hk. AE, MC, V. MTR: Central. Map p 56.*

Books

★ Dymocks Booksellers CENTRAL   This Australian chain always has a thorough selection of new releases and books about Hong Kong and China. It's not as sleek as Page One or as funky as Swindon, but it's got a good magazine selection and plenty of airplane reading. *Shop 2007–2011, IFC Mall, 8 Finance St.* ☎ *852/2117-0360. www.dymocks. com. AE, DC, MC, V. MTR: Central. Map p 56.*

★★ Page One CENTRAL   Page One stocks both Hong Kong books

Some of Hong Kong's hottest young artists show their work at Plum Blossoms.

Wah Tung China Company sells ceramics ranging from small statues to oversize floor vases.

for the coffee table and Western titles for the plane trip, as well as greeting cards, notebooks, and journals. *Century Square, 1–13 D'Aguilar St. ☎ 852/2536-0111. www.page onegroup.com. AE, DC, MC, V. MTR: Central. Map p 56.*

★★★ Swindon Book Co. Ltd.
TSIM SHA TSUI   You'll find everything from pocket Cantonese phrase books to magazines from the U.S. and U.K. at this sprawling bookstore.

Founded in 1918, it has the feel of an old library, with large stacks and a huge selection of new and used books. *13–15 Lock Rd. ☎ 852/2366-8001. www.swindonbooks.com. AE, DC, MC, V. MTR: Tsim Sha Tsui. Map p 55.*

Carpets
★★ Chinese Carpet Centre
TSIM SHA TSUI   In business 30 years, this large showroom has a huge selection of both hand- and machine-woven Chinese carpets and stands out from the rest for its reasonable prices. *Shop 5, 63 Mody Rd. ☎ 852/2730-7230. www.cccrugs. com.hk. AE, DC, MC, V. MTR: Tsim Sha Tsui. Map p 55.*

★★★ Mir Oriental Carpets CEN-
TRAL   Mir offers some great deals on Oriental rugs—hand-knotted Persian rugs from Pakistan start at around \$HK23,400—though antique rugs sell for up to \$HK156,000. *New India House, 52 Wyndham St. ☎ 852/2521-5641. www.miroriental carpets.com. AE, DC, MC, V. Bus: 13, 26, or 40M. Map p 56.*

Ceramics & Glass
★★ Overjoy KWAI CHUNG   You
have to take a taxi from the MTR

For Chinese-made rugs that look great on the floor or as wall hangings, head to the Chinese Carpet Centre.

If you're looking to stock up on Chinese items, Yue Hwa will have just what you're looking for.

stop to get here, but the payoff is a huge selection of inexpensive, quality porcelain; table settings are their specialty. You can commission a set using either one of their 400 designs or one of your own, and the prices are the best in town. *Kwai Hing Industrial Building, 10–18 Chun Pin St., Block B,* ☎ *852/2511-2763. AE, MC, V. MTR: Kwai Hing Station, then taxi. Map p 55.*

★ Wah Tung China Company

CENTRAL   Wah Tung offers a wide selection of Chinese hand-painted ceramics and pieces from various dynastic periods. It also sells European makes and designs, though why buy those in China? *59 Hollywood Rd.* ☎ *852/2543-2823. www.wahtungchina.com. AE, DC, MC, V. MTR: Central. Bus: 26. Map p 56.*

Chinese Emporiums
★★ Chinese Arts & Crafts

TSIM SHA TSUI   The prices here are high, but so is the quality of the goods. You'll find Chinese silk dresses, jade jewelry, and Chinese herbs and tea. Items are clearly labeled, the staff is knowledgeable, and the store is large and easy to navigate. *Star House, 3 Salisbury Rd.*

☎ *852/2735-4061. www.crcretail. com. AE, DC, MC, V. MTR: Tsim Sha Tsui. Map p 55.*

★ Yue Hwa Chinese Products

CANAL BELT   This chain is as close to mainland Chinese shopping as you can get in Hong Kong—it's packed with such unusual Chinese goods as snake wine, which comes with an actual snake in the bottle. The items here are of lesser quality than Chinese Arts & Crafts (see "Chinese Arts & Crafts," above), but they're also cheaper. *G/F–3/F, No. 1 Kowloon Park Dr.* ☎ *852/2317-5333. www.yuehwa. com. AE, MC, V. MTR: Tsim Sha Tsui. Map p 55.*

Electronics & Photography Equipment
★ Apliu Street SHAM SHIU PO

A street market packed with second-hand electronics, ranging from cell-phones to video game consoles, worked back into shape by some of Hong Kong's many electronics aficionados. Best to stick to small ticket items, as some goods may not have a long lifespan and there are no warrantees. *MTR: Sham Shui Po. Map p 55.*

★★ Star Computer City TSIM

SHA TSUI   Hong Kong is a computer

Apliu Street is a techno geek's dream come true.

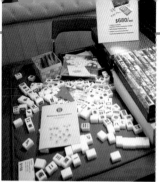

Stock up on mahjong sets while you hunt for fashion finds at G.O.D.

and gadget lover's town, and this is a good place to dive into the offerings, with a large variety of individual shops selling laptops, PCs, computer screens, and MP3 players. Since everything is piled together, it can be a little tricky to find what you want, so give yourself time to explore. *3 Salisbury Rd.* ☎ *852/2736-2608. Many shops take AE, MC, V. MTR: Tsim Sha Tsui. Map p 55.*

★★★ Wan Chai Computer Centre WAN CHAI
I'm writing this book on a laptop I bought at this crowded, messy, and very cheap electronics center. It can be claustrophobic, but it's worth it if you're looking for great deals. *130 Hennessy Rd. Many shops take AE, MC, V. MTR: Wan Chai. Map p 56.*

Fashion

★★ agnès b. CENTRAL
This is the Hong Kong outlet of the French fashion designer, popular with locals for her simple but elegant clothing for women and men. *Shop 1098, 2088–2089, IFC.* ☎ *852/2805-0611. www.agnesb.com. AE, DC, MC, V. MTR: Central. Map p 56.*

★★★ Blanc de Chine CENTRAL
This stylish, Chinese-influenced clothing line features elegant silk dresses, jackets with Chinese characters, and jewelry. *Shop 201–203A,*

12 Pedder St. ☎ *852/2524-7875. www.blancdechine.com. AE, DC, MC, V. MTR: Central. Map p 56.*

★★ D-Mop CAUSEWAY BAY
A popular label specializing in urban street wear, hip-hop attire, and other garb you'll see on Hong Kong's younger residents. *Shop B, Greenfield Mansion, 8 Kingston St.* ☎ *852/2203-4130. AE, DC, MC, V. MTR: Causeway Bay. Map p 56.*

★★★ G.O.D. CAUSEWAY BAY
The initials stand for "Goods of Desire," and even when I stop in with the intention of just window-shopping, I usually can't resist. There's a lot to choose from: clothes, CDs, funky furniture, small gifts, and cards. *Leighton Centre, Sharp St. E.* ☎ *852/2524-5555. www.god.com.hk. AE, DC, MC, V. MTR: Causeway Bay. Map p 56.*

★★ Joyce Boutique CENTRAL
Joyce Boutique is a well-known chain selling designer brands like Yves Saint Laurent and Issey Miyake at reasonable prices. Joyce Ma started the store in the 1970s to bring European fashion to Hong Kong women, but now she also

The founder of Joyce Boutique helped introduce European fashions to Hong Kong.

Designer David Tang made traditional Chinese styles hip—fashionistas flock to Shanghai Tang for his gear.

showcases Asian and local designers. *18 Queen's Rd.* ☎ *852/2810-1120. AE, DC, MC, V. MTR: Central. Map p 56.*

★★★ **Shanghai Tang** CENTRAL When founder David Tang launched his clothing line in 1994, his goal was to make traditional Chinese clothing—collarless shirts, loose-fitting pants—stylish and modern. He now has stores in New York, Paris, and London selling his chic designs for men and women. Buy off the rack or get custom tailoring. *12 Pedder St.* ☎ *852/2525-7333. www.shanghaitang.com. AE, DC, MC, V. MTR: Central. Map p 56.*

★ **Vivienne Tam** CENTRAL One of China's best-known designers, Vivienne Tam now sells her funky fashions worldwide, but she got her start here in Hong Kong. This cool boutique carries her entire line. *Shop 2095, IFC Mall.* ☎ *852/2868-9268. www.viviennetam.com. AE, DC, MC, V. MTR: Central. Map p 56.*

Jewelry
★★ **King Fook Jewelry** CENTRAL King Fook has been selling consumer brand women's and men's

jewelry, watches, and pens by makers like Christine Dior, Tag Heuer, and Gucci since 1949. There's a lot to choose from here, and the staff is especially friendly. *30–32 Des Voeux Rd.* ☎ *852/2822-8573. AE, DC, MC, V. www.kingfook.com. MTR: Central. Map p 56.*

★★ **The Opal Mine** TSIM SHA TSUI Billed as Hong Kong's "only opal cave shop," the interior of this store really does look cavelike. They specialize in both refined opal jewelry and raw opals. *Shop G, Burlington House, 92 Nathan Rd.* ☎ *852/2721-9933. www.opalnet.com. AE, MC, V. MTR: Tsim Sha Tsui. Map p 55.*

★ **Oriental Arts Jewelry** TSHIM SHA TSUI There's an excellent selection of jade and other jewelry at this elegant shop in the Peninsula Hotel. It's also the perfect stop for those who like to make their own jewelry, as there are a number of loose items (like beads and stones) to choose from. *The Peninsula Hotel, Salisbury Rd.* ☎ *852/2369-0820. AE, DC, MC, V. MTR: Tsim Sha Tsui. Map p 55.*

Oriental Arts shows off some of its finest wares.

Malls & Department Stores

★ **Harbour City** TSIM SHA TSUI
Before mainland China started
opening megamalls, this one was
billed as the biggest in Asia. With
more than 700 stores, it's a huge
draw for both mainland and Western
visitors, making it one of Hong
Kong's best people-watching spots.
Canton Rd. ☎ *852/2118-8601. www.
harbourcity.com.hk. Most shops take
AE, DC, MC, V. MTR: Tsim Sha Tsui.
Map p 55.*

★★★ **IFC Mall** CENTRAL This
sleek mall in the center of the city
has high-end shops, a movie theater, restaurants, and bars. It also
connects to the Mid-Levels escalator
so it's within easy reach of Lan Kwai
Fong and SoHo. *8 Finance St.* ☎ *852/
2295-3308. www.ifc.com.hk. Most
shops take AE, DC, MC, V. MTR: Central. Map p 56.*

★★ **Lane Crawford** ADMIRALTY
A Hong Kong landmark, Lane Crawford was founded in 1850 and offers
designer labels, cosmetics, and jewelry from around the world. Before
the influx of international brands, it
was *the* place to go for Western
styles, and it's still popular with

*The cool, calm Pacific Place mall offers a
refreshing break from market shopping.*

*The quality may not always be top-notch,
but the jewelry on sale at the Jade Market is still very pretty.*

locals for its gallery-like rooms and
elegant restaurants. *88 Queensway.*
☎ *852/2118-3668. AE, DC, MC, V.
MTR: Admiralty. Map p 56.*

★★★ **Pacific Place** ADMIRALTY
The best thing about this mall is the
sweeping, curved interior. The high-end goods (think Prada, Dior, Louis
Vuitton) are an added bonus. With a
plethora of shops, grocery stores,
and restaurants, it's easy to spend
an afternoon here. *88 Queensway.*
☎ *852/2844-8988. www.pacific
place.com.hk. Most shops take AE,
DC, MC, V. MTR: Causeway Bay. Map
p 56.*

★ **Sogo** CAUSEWAY BAY This
large, often-crowded Japanese
department store is popular with
locals. It carries clothing, toys,
household goods, and electronics at
competitive prices. *555 Hennessy
Rd.* ☎ *852/3556-1212. www.sogo.
com.hk. AE, DC, MC, V. MTR: Causeway Bay. Map p 56.*

★★ **Times Square** CAUSEWAY
BAY Located at the center of
bustling Times Square, this mall is a
good place if you're looking for reasonably priced Western-style duds.
Stores include Timberland, Nike,
and the U.K.'s Marks & Spencer.
1 Matheson St. ☎ *852/2118-8900.
www.timessquare.com.hk. Most
shops take AE, DC, MC, V. MTR:
Causeway Bay. Map p 56.*

Markers

★ Cat Street SHEUNG WAN

I love browsing this quaint street because of the relaxed atmosphere. It's also a great place to find cheap Mao paraphernalia—his image adorns everything from buttons to watches and clocks—as well as Chinese compasses, calligraphy brushes, and 1960s-era prints of Chinese laborers. *Upper Lascar Row. No credit cards on the street. MTR: Sheung Wan. Map p 56.*

★★ Jade Market YAU MA TEI

China is famous for jade jewelry and art, and you can find small items at low prices here, though you'll need to bargain for the best deals. But buyer beware: Big ticket items at this market sometimes turn out to be rip-offs. *Between Kansu and Battery sts. Some sellers take AE, MC, V. MTR: Jordan. Map p 55.*

★★ Ladies' Market MONG KOK

A bustling market where you can buy your fill of Chinese "rip-off" versions of designer handbags, sunglasses, and watches. It can be very crowded, so plan to spend at least an hour. *Tung Choi St. between Argyle and Dundas. No credit cards on the street. MTR: Mong Kok. Map p 55.*

★ Stanley Market STANLEY VIL-

LAGE   Although this was once a great place for bargains, it's a bit of a tourist trap now. Still, it's worth a visit if you're in the market for silk clothing. *Main St. Some shops take AE, MC, V. Bus: 6, 6A, 6X, or 260 from Exchange Square in Central; 973 from Mody Rd in Tsim Sha Tsui East. Map p 56.*

★★★ Temple Street Night

Market YAU MA TEI   With hundreds of vendors selling everything from cheap CDs to handbags, this is one of Hong Kong's liveliest markets. It's also famous for its food stalls, where you can get good,

cheap fried seafood on the go. *Temple St. MTR: Jordan. Map p 55.*

Medicine

★★★ Eu Yan Sang CENTRAL

This chain is a foreigner-friendly place to buy Chinese medicine (see "Chinese Medicine," p 51). The staff speaks English and is eager to help you make your selections. *152–156 Queen's Rd. ☎ 852/2544-3870. www.euyansang.com. AE, MC, V. MTR: Central. Map p 56.*

Sporting Goods

★★ Giga Sports TSIM SHA TSUI

Giga is one of the few places in Hong Kong where you can find a large selection of gear for outdoor sports activities such as hiking, running, or swimming. *Ocean Terminal, Harbour City, Canton Rd. ☎ 852/2115-9930. AE, DC, MC, V. MTR: Tsim Sha Tsui; Star Ferry terminal. Map p 55.*

Tailors

★★ A-Man Hing Cheong Co.

Ltd. CENTRAL   This Hong Kong tailor makes shirts and suits with a European cut, making it popular among expatriates from the U.K. *Mandarin Oriental Hotel, 5 Connaught Rd.*

Shop for accessories at the Ladies' Market.

☎ 852/2522-3336. AE, DC, MC, V. MTR: Central. Map p 56.

★ **Grand Tailors** TSIM SHA TSUI They've been around for decades, and have an excellent staff who will ensure you get your suit or shirts exactly as you want them. It's not the cheapest place to go, but it's reliable. *VIP Commercial Centre, 120 Canton Rd., 7th Floor.* ☎ 852/2302-4444. www.grandtailors.com. AE, DC, MC, V. MTR: Tsim Sha Tsui. Map p 55.

★★★ **Raja Fashions** TSIM SHA TSUI The staff here is patient and thoughtful, which comes in handy when you're confronted with having to choose from over 20,000 kinds of fabric. *34-C Cameron Rd.* ☎ 852/2366-1801. www.raja-fashions.com. AE, DC, MC, V. MTR: Tsim Sha Tsui. Map p 55.

★★★ **Sam's Tailor** TSIM SHA TSUI The most famous tailor in Hong Kong, Sam's has made clothing for everyone from former British prime minister Tony Blair to tennis star Serena Williams. You can find cheaper tailors in Hong Kong, but you won't get that Sam's quality. *Shop K, Burlington Arcade, 92–94 Nathan Rd.* ☎ 852/2367-9423.

www.samstailor.com. AE, DC, MC, V. MTR: Tsim Sha Tsui. Map p 55.

Tea & Tea Sets

★★ **Fook Ming Tong** CENTRAL This shop blends its own tea and let's you take a taste to help you decide what to buy. Teapots, teacups, and tea caddies are all available. *1 Duddell St.,* ☎ 852/2521-8626. AE, MC, V. MTR: Central. Map p 56.

★★★ **Lock Cha Tea Shop** SHEUNG WAN The staff here can help you select the perfect tea— and can teach you the proper way to pour it. They carry peony white tea, which is popular in Hong Kong and served in many of the restaurants in the city. *Upper Ground Floor, 290A, Queens' Rd.* ☎ 852/2805-1360. www.lockcha.com. AE, MC, V. MTR: Sheung Wan. Map p 56.

Toys

★★ **kids Toy Museum** CENTRAL If your child needs a new toy for the plane trip home, this kid-friendly store has loads of options, including dolls, action figures, and Pokemon. *Shop 320, 10 Chater Rd.* ☎ 852/2869-9138. AE, DC, MC, V. MTR: Central. Map p 56.

★ **kids Wise Kids** ADMIRALTY The very idea of nonelectronic toys is hard to imagine in Hong Kong, where even adults play video games on the MTR. But this shop sells toys (like puzzles and board games) that don't involve batteries or LCD screens. *Shop 134, Pacific Place, 88 Queensway.* ☎ 852/2868-0133. AE, MC, V. MTR: Admiralty. Map p 56. ●

Stop in at Fook Ming Tong to try their specially blended teas.

Hong Kong **Beaches**

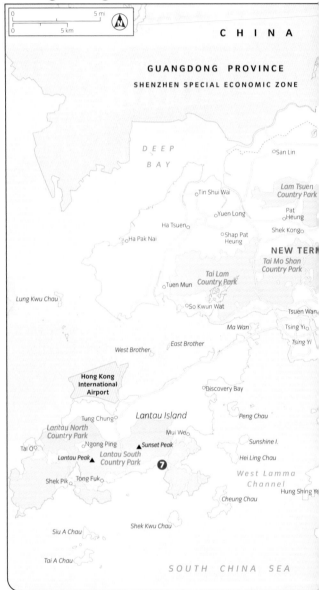

CHINA

GUANGDONG PROVINCE

SHENZHEN SPECIAL ECONOMIC ZONE

DEEP BAY

San Lin

Lam Tsuen Country Park

Tin Shui Wai

Yuen Long

Pat Heung

Ha Tsuen

Shap Pat Heung

Shek Kong

Ha Pak Nai

NEW TERR

Tai Mo Shan Country Park

Tai Lam Country Park

Tuen Mun

Lung Kwu Chau

So Kwun Wat

Tsuen Wan

Ma Wan

Tsing Yi

Tsing Yi

West Brother

East Brother

Hong Kong International Airport

Discovery Bay

Peng Chau

Tung Chung

Lantau Island

Lantau North Country Park

Ngong Ping

Mui Wo

Sunshine I.

Tai O

▲ Sunset Peak

Lantau Peak ▲

Lantau South Country Park

Hei Ling Chau

❼

Shek Pik

Tong Fuk

West Lamma Channel

Cheung Chau

Hung Shing Ye

Siu A Chau

Shek Kwu Chau

Tai A Chau

SOUTH CHINA SEA

Previous page: A huge statue of Tin Hau on Repulse Bay Beach.

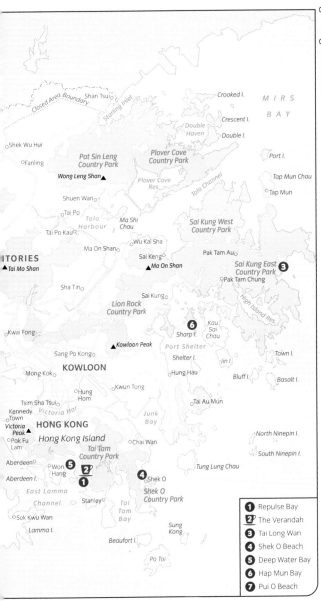

1	Repulse Bay
2	The Verandah
3	Tai Long Wan
4	Shek O Beach
5	Deep Water Bay
6	Hap Mun Bay
7	Pui O Beach

There are about 40 free public beaches in and around Hong Kong, and they differ widely in terms of cleanliness, views, and access to swimming. Since Hong Kong is almost always hot, and the city can get claustrophobic, you'll likely want to visit at least one of these beaches, so I've suggested a day trip that includes two of my favorites, along with a list of the best of the rest. Keep in mind that most beaches have changing rooms, snack stands or restaurants, and lifeguards on duty from April to October. Beware of pollution which can be a problem depending on the tides and time of year.

START: **Exchange Square bus terminal in Central.**

---

1 ★ **Repulse Bay.** This is the quintessential Hong Kong beach, lined with high-end apartment complexes, beachfront restaurants, and large facilities for changing and showering. It also features massive statues of Chinese gods (including, of course, Tin Hau, goddess of the sea). The beach's name is quite literal, as it refers to the way the British "repulsed" pirates from the shore in the mid-1800s. Come early in the day, before the masses of city dwellers descend for their afternoon swim. ⏱ *3 hr. Bus: 6, 6A, 6X, or 260.*

This enormous statue of a Chinese goddess is just one of many that make up an outdoor temple at Repulse Bay.

When you're ready for a break from the sun and sand, head to **2** ★ **The Verandah.** The dining room has high ceilings with fans whirling softly, and windows overlooking beautifully landscaped lawns with the beach and ocean beyond. The menu offers grilled fish, meat, and seafood, like lobster and crab. *109 Repulse Bay Rd.* ☎ *852/2812-2722. $$$.*

3 ★★★ **Tai Long Wan (Big Wave Bay).** Though it takes some effort to reach this secluded, serene set of connected beaches, they're by far the best in the city. Wide swaths of sand are backed by rolling green hills and rocky ridges and there is a small cafe at the far end of the beach where you can get drinks, food, or change your clothes. If you're in the mood, there's a trail leading to several more beaches. ⏱ *5 hr. Tai Long Wan. MTR: Choi Hung,*

High-rise apartment buildings line the hills around Repulse Bay.

Skim boarding is a popular pastime on Hong Kong's beaches.

to any minibus with "Sai Kung" written on the front, then take a 20-min taxi ride to "Tai Long Sai Wan." Follow the path to the beach.

Other Great Beaches

4 Shek O. Although this beach is relatively close to the city, on the south side of the island, it still manages to feel like it's a world away from anything remotely urban. Shek O, which means "rocky bay," has beautiful scenery thanks to the surrounding cliffs, which are indeed rocky. *MTR: Shau Kei Wan, then bus 9.*

5 Deep Water Bay. Deep Water Bay is adjacent to Repulse Bay (see "Repulse Bay," above)—they're connected via the Seaview Promenade, an easy walking path. Its popularity likely has much to do with its proximity to the city, but the views of the surrounding hills don't hurt either. The water here is not as clean as spots farther from downtown, but it's usually safe for swimming. *Bus: 6 or 6X from Central.*

6 Hap Mun Bay. If you're planning to head to Sai Kung for a delicious and ridiculously fresh seafood dinner, consider spending the afternoon at Hap Mun Bay. You can catch a sampan from Sai Kung, and the ride to this impeccably clean spot is part of the fun. It's very popular with

locals, and the crowd is lively but not terribly loud. You can watch the ferries make their way across the harbor in the distance. *MTR: Diamond Hill, then bus 92 to Sai Kung. Sampan drivers will be easy to spot and offer round-trip rides.*

7 Pui O. If you like crowds, this is the spot for you. Pui O, on Lantau, gets very busy, though it's still often possible to find open spots at the far end of the beach if you want a little alone time. There is a restaurant right on the beach that serves drinks and snacks. *Ferry from Central to Lantau, then anybus leaving Mui Wo. Tell the driver you'd like to get off at Pui O.*

Locals and visitors alike enjoy the sunny skies and warm waters of Shek O beach.

Hong Kong **Hikes**

CHINA

GUANGDONG PROVINCE

SHENZHEN SPECIAL ECONOMIC ZONE

DEEP BAY

San Lin

Lam Tsuen Country Park

Tin Shui Wai

Yuen Long

Pat Heung

Shek Kong

NEW TERR

Ha Tsuen

Shap Pat Heung

Tai Mo Shan Country Park

Ha Pak Nai

Tai Lam Country Park

Tuen Mun

So Kwun Wat

Tsuen Wan

Lung Kwu Chau

Ma Wan

Tsing Yi

Tsing Yi

East Brother

West Brother

Hong Kong International Airport

Discovery Bay

Tung Chung

Lantau Island

Peng Chau

Lantau North Country Park

Ngong Ping

Mui Wo

Sunshine I.

Tai O

Sunset Peak ⑥

Hei Ling Chau

Lantau Peak

Lantau South Country Park

West Lamma Channel

Shek Pik

Tong Fuk

Hung Shing Ye

Cheung Chau

Siu A Chau

Shek Kwu Chau

Tai A Chau

SOUTH CHINA SEA

0   5 mi
0   5 km

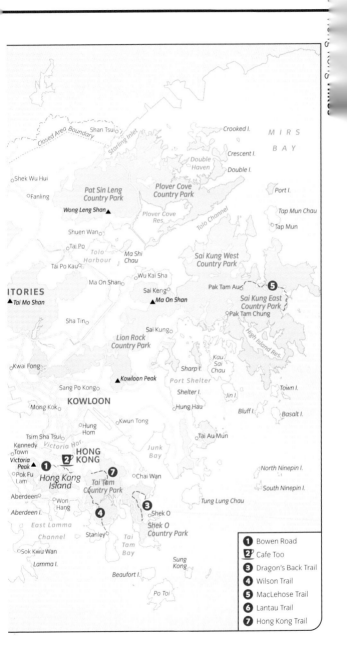

1 Bowen Road
2 Cafe Too
3 Dragon's Back Trail
4 Wilson Trail
5 MacLehose Trail
6 Lantau Trail
7 Hong Kong Trail

Hong Kong's natural beauty often comes as a surprise to visitors, who tend to think of the city as a crowded urban center. In fact, due to government oversight and control of land, about 70% of Hong Kong is undeveloped. This section gives you a day trip that starts with a leisurely walk on Hong Kong Island, leads to a more strenuous hike on the island's south side, and ends at a beach in the seaside village of Sai Kung. It also lists some of the best short hikes in Hong Kong. In summertime, the weather can get extremely hot, so be prepared by bringing water, food, and the proper clothing. START: **Magazine Gap Road, near Peak Tram.**

1 ★★ **kids** **Bowen Road.** This tree-lined road was named in honor of Hong Kong's ninth governor, George Ferguson Bowen, and it's an easy, paved 4km (2.5-mile) route. After some not so impressive terrain, Bowen becomes an elevated path shaded by a canopy of trees. To your left is the city and harbor. Farther on, you'll pass through Wan Chai (the neighborhood that served as the setting for the movie *The World of Suzie Wong*) before ending at Happy Valley, where Bowen merges with Stubbs Road, and where you'll find a number of small ancestral shrines, playgrounds, and hillside mansions. 🕐 **90 min. Bowen Rd. MTR: Central.**

Before you begin your second walk, stop in at **2** ★★ **Cafe Too** in the Island Shangri-La Hotel. There's a lot

The stunning views from Dragon's Back include this look down at Shek O beach.

to choose from at this casual food hall: Options are laid out buffet style at seven separate stations and include sushi, Peking duck, dim sum, and pizza. *Island Shangri-La Hong Kong, Pacific Place.* ☎ 852/2820-8571. $$.

3 ★★★ **Dragon's Back.** Your second walk is also 4km (2.5 miles) long, but it's a completely different experience from relatively urban Bowen Road. The somewhat strenuous Dragon's Back trail rises dramatically along the D'Augilar Peninsula, beginning rather inauspiciously at the Tai Tam Correctional Institute. Stick to it and you'll soon enter a shady green forest dotted with small streams, emerging to find spectacular views of Big Wave Bay, the islands, and Stanley Peninsula before descending into bamboo groves. You'll end near lovely Shek O beach (see "Shek O," p 71). 🕐 **2 hr. Dragon's Back Trail. MTR: Shau Kei Wan to bus 9, get off at Big Wave Bay.**

A stone lion marks the way along Bowen Road.

Trek Smart

Hong Kong is a surprisingly hiker-friendly city. The government-run **Map Publications Centre** (North Point Government Offices, 333 Java Rd.; ☎ 852/2231-3187) offers free maps of most of the city's trails. I also recommend picking up *Hong Kong Hikes: The Twenty Best Walks in the Territory* by Christian Wright and Tinja Tsang, which features laminated maps. Since the weather in Hong Kong can range from very hot to very rainy, you should bring both water and a light rain jacket on any trek you plan to take. And while the trails around Hong Kong are generally safe, it's always smart to let someone (like the concierge at your hotel) know what your plans are. If you don't want to go it alone, there are a number of options for guided hikes (see "Guide My Way," p 76).

Other Great Hikes

4 Wilson Trail. This rugged hike starts out slowly before reaching concrete steps that take you up to the summit of the Twins, the two-pronged peak overlooking Stanley (386m/1,266 ft.). You can either climb the Twins or go around them, after which you'll descend to the Repulse Bay Pass, before reaching Violet Hills. On a clear day, you'll be able to see all the way to Lamma. This part of the trail (which is much longer) ends at the Wong Nai Chung Reservoir. ⏱ *2 hr. Bus: 6, 6X, 73 or 260 or green minibus: 16M or 40 to Wilson Trail on Stanley Gap Rd.*

5 ★★ MacLehose Trail. It's a long and sometimes difficult hike, but it takes you along the gorgeous coastline of Sai Kung to Tai Long Wan beach, one of the best in Hong Kong (see "Tai Long Wan [Big Wave Bay]," p 70). ⏱ *5 hr. MTR: to Diamond Hill, then bus 92 to Sai Kung Village. Change to bus 94 to Wong Shek Pier, which will take you to Pak Tam Au, where the hike begins.*

6 Lantau Trail. Sunset Peak and Lantau Peak are the highlights of this hike, which involves some strenuous climbs. But the views—of Lantau's beaches, among other

A hiker makes his way along the Tai Long Wan beach stretch of the MacLehose Trail.

Mist enshrouds part of the Lantau Trail, which winds its way along Lantau Island's rolling green hills.

things—are worth it. Not only that, but this section of the trail (the whole thing is 70km/43 miles) is nearly always crowd free, even on the weekends. *5 hr. Ferry from Central to Mui Wo on Lantau. Take bus 1, 3, or 3M and get off at Nam Shan. Walk to the Nam Shan Country Park Management Centre, where the trail begins.*

7 Hong Kong Trail. This is the perfect hike for those who want a little light exercise but don't want to spend their day huffing and puffing. It's a relatively easy walk with beautiful views of Hong Kong and the surrounding islands. The top of Mount Butler is a great viewpoint to see the city, harbor, and the Tai Tam reservoir, all from one spot. There are multiple exit points along the trail, in case you get tired of walking. *3 hr. Bus 6 or 61 to the Shell petrol station at Parkview. Walk up the stairs beside the station to Tai Tam Reservoir Rd; continue uphill for about 10 min. to the start of the trail.* ●

Guide My Way

There's so much to see along Hong Kong's green trails that it would be a shame to skip taking a hike because you're nervous about heading out alone. Happily, there are a number of options for excellent guided hikes and nature walks (Hong Kong is home to 450 species of birds, for example). **Hong Kong Trampers** (☎ 852/8209-0517; www.hktrampers.com) is a friendly, casual group that organizes weekly hiking trips to various spots around the island. **Outdoor Adventure Tours** (☎ 852/9300-5197; www.kayak-and-hike.com) leads some excellent hikes in addition to running full-day kayaking trips to both the islands and the New Territories to see volcanic beaches and coral arches. Prices vary depending on the trip. Another trustworthy tour group is **Dragonfly** (☎ 852/2916-8230; www.dragonfly.com.hk), which offers a variety of tours, including rock climbing, caving, and mountain biking trips.

Dining Best Bets

Best Roast Goose
★★★ Yung Kee Restaurant $$
32–40 Wellington St. (p 90)

Best Private Kitchen
★★★ Da Ping Huo $$ *49 Hollywood Rd. (p 84)*

Best Japanese
★★★ Wasabisabi $$$ *1 Matheson St. (p 90)*

Best Frog
★★ Fook Lam Moon $$ *53–59 Kimberley Rd. (p 85)*

Best Dim Sum
★★★ Luk Yu Teahouse $$
24–26 Stanley St. (p 86)

Best Italian Seafood
★★ Anthony's Catch $$$
Po Tung Rd. (p 83)

Best Floating Restaurant
★ Jumbo Kingdom $$$ *Aberdeen Harbour (p 86)*

Best View of Hong Kong Island
★★ Hutong $$$ *1 Peking Rd. (p 86)*

Best Elegant Dim Sum Dining
★★★ Lung King Heen $$$
8 Finance St. (p 86)

Best Vegetarian Chinese
★★★ Kung Tak Lam $$
31 Yee Wo St. (p 86)

Best Local Seafood
★★ Super Star Seafood Restaurant $$ *83–97 Nathan Rd. (p 89)*

Best Mexican
★★ Agave $$ *93–107 Lockhart Rd. (p 83)*

Best Dumplings
★★★ Peking Dumpling Wong $$$$
Shop D/F 118 Jaffe Rd. (p 88)

Best French Food
★★★ Spoon $$$ *18 Salisbury Rd. (p 89)*

Best Organic Fare
★★ Life $$ *10 Shelley St.*

Best Western-Food Fix
★ California Pizza Kitchen $
1 Matheson St. (p 83)

Best Beach Dining
★★ The Stoep $$ *32 Lower Cheung Sha Village (p 89)*

Chilli N Spice serves up some of the best Asian fusion food in town. See p 84.

Kowloon Dining

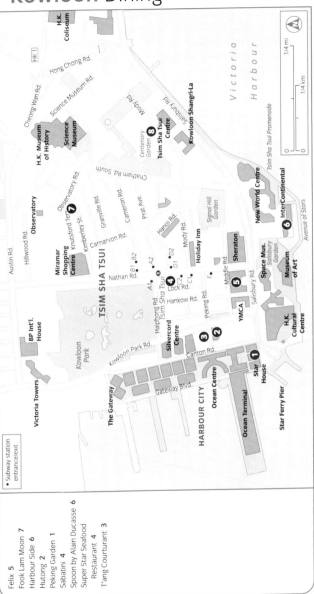

Felix **5**
Fook Lam Moon **7**
Harbour Side **6**
Hutong **2**
Peking Garden **1**
Sabatini **4**
Spoon by Alain Ducasse **6**
Super Star Seafood
Restaurant **4**
T'ang Courturant **3**

Photo p 77: Dim sum from trolleys at Maxim's Palace.

Central Dining

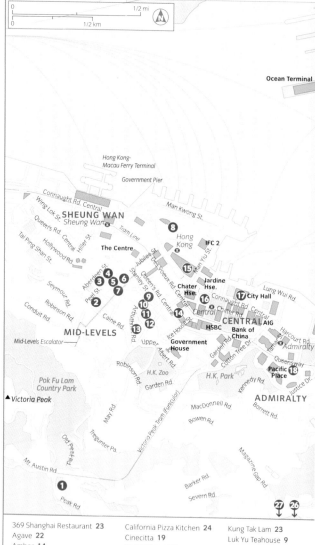

Maxim's Palace **17**
Mum Chau's Sichuan Kitchen **11**
One Harbour Road **20**
Peking Dumpling Wong **21**
Shui Huju **2**

Song **4**
The Square **15**
Thai Basil **18**
Tribute **3**
Veda **13**

Wasabisabi **24**
Yellow Door Kitchen **6**
Yung Kee Restaurant **9**

Sai Kung/Lamma/Lantau Dining

Anthony's Catch **3**
Rainbow Seafood Restaurant **2**
The Stoep **1**
Tung Kee Seafood Restaurant **3**

Restaurants A to Z

★ **Agave** WAN CHAI *MEXICAN* Decent Mexican is hard to find in Asia, so Agave's sizzling fajitas and chunky guacamole are a treat. The clientele is lively, thanks in part to the 150 tequilas on offer, and the street-side views are perfect for people-watching. *93–107 Lockhart Rd.* ☎ *852/2521-2010. Entrees $HK130–$HK180. AE, DC, MC, V. Lunch & dinner daily. MTR: Wanchai. Map p 80.*

★★★ **Amber** CENTRAL *EUROPEAN* Amber has ceiling art that looks a bit like long needles that dangle over diners. The food is as creative as the setting, with pistachio and apricot samosas, seared blue fin tuna cubes glazed with soy and maple, and for dessert, caramel, sea salt, and milk fondant with caramelized peanuts. *15 Queen's Rd.* ☎ *852/2132-0188. Entrees $HK300–$HK500. AE, DC, MC, V. Breakfast, lunch & dinner daily. MTR: Central. Map p 80.*

★★ **Anthony's Catch** SAI KUNG *ITALIAN/SEAFOOD* This small spot in the beach village of Sai Kung

At Amber, the ceiling art is almost as impressive as the menu.

offers up dishes with fish imported from Australia and New Zealand and ingredients brought in from Italy by chef Anthony Blair Sweet. In short, it's the kind of eatery you won't find anywhere but Hong Kong. *G/F 1826B Po Tung Rd.* ☎ *852/2792-8474. Entrees $HK130–$HK250. AE, MC, V. Lunch & dinner daily. MTR: Diamond Hill, exit C. Bus: 92. Map p 82.*

★★ **Café Deco** VICTORIA PEAK *INTERNATIONAL* Oddly, many of the Peak's restaurants don't have great views. Café Deco is the exception—it's an airy space with windows overlooking the city. The food ranges from French to Japanese and while it won't blow you away, the view certainly will. *Peak Galleria, Victoria Peak.* ☎ *852/2849-5111. Entrees $HK108–$HK248. AE, DC, MC, V. Lunch & dinner Mon–Fri; breakfast, lunch & dinner Sat–Sun. Peak tram. Map p 80.*

★ **Cafe Siam** SOHO *THAI* While there's plenty of good Thai food in Hong Kong, this quaint restaurant right off the Mid-Levels escalator has outstanding curries and staples such as pad thai at reasonable prices. There's a cozy downstairs and a more spacious second floor where you can see the street-scene below. *40–42 Lyndhurst Terrace.* ☎ *852/2851-4803. Entrees HK$68–HK$158. AE, MC, V. Lunch & dinner daily. MTR: Central to Mid-Levels escalator. Map p 80.*

★ **kids** **California Pizza Kitchen** CAUSEWAY BAY *PIZZA* If you have a hankering for Western food, but still want a taste of Asia, this chain offers up Peking duck pizza alongside its cheese and tomato pie. The atmosphere, though, is decidedly Western, with large tables and fast service. *Food Forum, 1 Matheson*

The view of the Hong Kong skyline is stunning from Hutong's chic dining room. See p 86.

St., 13th Floor, ☎ 852/3102-9132. Entrees $HK72–$HK108. AE, DC, MC, V. Lunch & dinner daily. MTR: Causeway Bay. Map p 80.

★★ **Chilli N Spice** STANLEY *ASIAN* This lounge-like restaurant, overlooking the water in Stanley, offers excellent Asian fusion cuisine in a relaxed atmosphere. The menu, which includes dishes like Singaporean-style fried curry crab and Indonesian curry chicken, has something for everyone. *Shop 101, Murray House.* ☎ 852/2899-0147. $$.

★★★ **Cinecitta** WAN CHAI *ITALIAN* A hip street in Wan Chai—on a rainy night, Star Street looks straight out of Wong Kar-wai's film, *In the Mood for Love*—is a surreal setting for great Italian food. But that's what you get at this chic, marble-floored restaurant, which features a glassed-in wine cellar. The bigoli with duck ragout is a restaurant specialty, as is the roast rack of lamb with

pistachio crust. Make reservations and plan to linger in the area after your meal, as equally funky 1/5 (listed in the nightlife chapter, p 100) is just down the street and is the perfect spot for a nightcap. *G/F 9 Star St.* ☎ 852/2539-0199. Entrees HK$100–HK$300. AE, DC, MC, V. Lunch & dinner daily. MTR: Wan Chai. Map p 80.

★ **kids Cococabana** DEEP WATER BAY *MEDITERRANEAN* This seaside spot has a European feel and great sunset views. Start with a selection of imported French cheeses, then try the restaurant specialty, Piri Piri prawns. Kids (and adults) can play on the beach before, during, and after dinner. *Upper G/F, Beach Building.* ☎ 852/2812-2226. Entrees $HK150–$HK250. AE, MC, V. Dinner Mon–Fri; lunch & dinner Sat–Sun. Bus: 6A, 6X, 41A, 65, 73, 76, 260, 315, 399, or 973. Map p 80.

★★★ **Da Ping Huo** CENTRAL *SICHUAN* One of Hong Kong's most popular private dining options, Da Ping Huo is run by a husband and wife team specializing in spicy Sichuan cuisine. Be prepared to eat, as meals consist of up to 14 courses, including Sichuan dumplings in garlic chili oil, spicy shrimp, and melon soup. The food is terrific, but the high point comes when the chef sings Chinese opera to guests at the end of the meal. *L/G 49 Hollywood Rd.* ☎ 852/2559-1317.

Private Dining

Private dining restaurants, where families open their homes and lay out set menus for patrons, are some of Hong Kong's best dining options. A not-so-well-kept secret, private kitchens first sprang up in the 1990s during the Asian financial crisis. While many of these places are humble in atmosphere, they often surpass four-star spots in terms of freshness, originality, and flavor; I've noted a few of the best in this chapter. Call a few days in advance for bookings.

Jumbo is like a theme-park version of a Chinese restaurant, complete with huge gold dragons lurking in the massive dining rooms. See p 86.

Set menu $HK250 per person. AE, DC, MC, V. MTR: Central. Map p 80.

★★★ **Felix** TSIM SHA TSUI *FUSION* The all-white interior of this Philippe Starck–designed restaurant competes with the spectacular view of Hong Kong Island (call ahead for a seat by the windows). The fusion food matches the funky setting, with dishes such as honeyed tempura prawns and Atlantic cod marinated with Japanese-misoyaki sauce, which are complimented by a large selection of French wines. *Peninsula Hotel, Salisbury Rd.* ☎ *852/2315-3188. Entrees $HK225–$HK350. AE, DC, MC, V. Dinner daily. MTR: Tsim Sha Tsui. Map p 79.*

★★ **Fook Lam Moon** TSIM SHA TSUI *CANTONESE* Pay homage to Hong Kong fare in all its glory at this large restaurant with large tables to accommodate large portions of braised shark's fin soup, deep-fried crispy chicken, and sweetened double-boiled bird's nest in fresh coconut. *53–59 Kimberley Rd.* ☎ *852/2366-0286. Entrees $HK100–$HK190. AE, DC, MC, V. Breakfast, lunch & dinner daily. MTR: Tsim Sha Tsui. Map p 79.*

★ kids **Harbour Side** TSIM SHA TSUI *INTERNATIONAL* This casual restaurant at the Hotel InterContinental features views of the harbor and Hong Kong Island from almost every table. It also offers a range of tasty delights for every palate, from juicy hamburgers to Asian classics like the Indonesian staple nasi goreng, a fried rice cooked with sweet soy sauce. The relaxed atmosphere makes it a great place for families. *Hotel InterContinental,*

You'll find old-fashioned Chinese favorites like spring rolls at Luk Yu Teahouse. See p 86.

Salisbury Rd. ☎ 852/2721-1211.
*Entrees HK$130–HK$350. AE, DC,
MC, V. Daily 6-12:30am. MTR: Tsim
Sha Tsui. Map p 79.*

★★ **Hutong** TSIM SHA TSUI
NORTHERN CHINESE The combination of rustic Chinese furniture and
floor-to-ceiling windows revealing
the harbor and skyline makes this an
enticing spot. The clientele is a bit
stuffy, but the menu makes up for it,
with excellent drunken raw crabs in
rice wine, braised veal shank in
osmanthus flower sauce, and an
extensive wine list. *1 Peking Rd.
☎ 852/3428-8342. Entrees $HK118–
$HK288; $HK300 minimum. AE, DC,
MC, V. Lunch & dinner daily. MTR:
Tsim Sha Tsui. Map p 79.*

★ **kids Jumbo Kingdom**
ABERDEEN SEAFOOD You take a
free shuttle past fishing junks to
arrive at this campy family eatery,
billed as the world's largest floating
restaurant. The menu features
seafood like fresh lobster salad and
Chinese dishes like Peking duck.
*Aberdeen Harbour. ☎ 852/2553-
9111. Entrees $HK80–$HK400. AE,
DC, MC, V. Breakfast, lunch & dinner
daily. Bus: 7 or 70 from Central, then
Jumbo's boat from pier. Map p 80.*

★★★ **Kung Tak Lam** CAUSEWAY
BAY SHANGHAINESE VEGETARIAN
Popular among vegetarians, this

*Dim sum is like tapas—lots of different
dishes served in small portions.*

*Noodle soups are a Hong Kong staple
and can be found at many restaurants.*

place is a win-win for those looking
to take a break from meat and still
get a taste of Shanghai cuisine.
Meat substitutes are used for dishes
such as mapo doufu, a spicy tofu
dish usually made with minced pork.
The restaurant is bright and airy and
has views of the harbor. *31 Yee Wo
St. ☎ 853/2890-3127. Entrees
$HK100–$HK250. AE, MC, V. Lunch &
dinner daily. MTR: Causeway Bay.
Map p 80.*

★★★ **Luk Yu Teahouse** CEN-
TRAL DIM SUM This teahouse has
been serving dim sum since 1933,
and the atmosphere, with its golden
colors and Chinese landscape paintings, is a blast from Hong Kong's
past. The food is some of the tasti-
est and freshest in town (try the
steamed rice wrapped in lotus
leaves). Come before 11am, when
the dim sum is still served by trolley,
but be prepared to wait. *24–26 Stanley St. ☎ 852/2523-5464. Entrees
$HK100–$HK220. MC, V. Breakfast,
lunch & dinner daily. MTR: Central.
Map p 80.*

★★★ **Lung King Heen** CENTRAL
CANTONESE With its elegant dining room, jade chopsticks, and fabu-
lous views, this is one of the best
hotel restaurants in town. The Cantonese cuisine is creatively done,
with dishes such as crispy glutinous
rice dumplings stuffed with beef

satay and steamed shrimp dumplings with bamboo. *8 Finance St.* ☎ *852/3196-8888. Entrees $HK68–$HK158. AE, DC, MC, V. Lunch & dinner daily. MTR: Central to Mid-levels escalator. Map p 80.*

★★★ **Mandarin Grill** CENTRAL *CONTINENTAL* The gleaming white interior of this popular hotel restaurant is flanked by an oyster bar with a long, wooden serving table. Once you've had a taste of the grilled tuna or the succulent Australian wagyu beef, you can take in the view of downtown Hong Kong. *5 Connaught Rd.* ☎ *852/2522-0111. Entrees $HK265–$HK440. AE, DC, MC, V. Breakfast, lunch & dinner daily. MTR: Central. Map p 80.*

★★ **M at the Fringe** CENTRAL *CONTINENTAL* With its curved tables and chairs, the dining room here may have you feeling a bit like you're inside a Salvador Dalí painting. The menu is creative, too, offering chargrilled pigeon with cannelini and pancetta stew, and potato gnocchi with sweetbreads. *2 Lower Albert Rd.* ☎ *852/2522-0111. Entrees $HK200–$HK250. AE, MC, V. Lunch & dinner Mon–Fri; dinner Sat–Sun. MTR: Central. Bus: 26. Map p 80.*

★★ **Maxim's Palace** CENTRAL *DIM SUM* Sprawling, cheap, and

Food is meant to be shared at traditional Chinese restaurants.

packed on Sundays, this is a can't-miss Hong Kong experience. Hong Kong families gather here to choose dim sum from rolling trolley carts (today, such service is increasingly rare). I recommend the fried squid tentacles and steamed pork buns. *Low Block, City Hall, Connaught Rd. Central and Edinburgh Place.* ☎ *852/2526-9931. Dim sum $HK17–$HK29. AE, DC, MC, V. Lunch Mon–Sat; breakfast & lunch Sun. MTR: Central. Map p 80.*

★★★ **Mum Chau's Sichuan Kitchen** CENTRAL *SICHUAN* This down-home Chinese restaurant has plastic tablecloths and chairs, but the mother-daughter team who runs it serves wonderfully spicy Sichuan dishes that include hand-thrown

An expert noodle maker plies his trade at Peking Garden. See p 88.

noodles in spicy sauce, homemade dumplings, and chicken flavored with star anise. *Winners Building, 37 D'Aguilar St., 7th Floor.* ☎ *852/8108-8550. Set menu $HK180. No credit cards. Lunch & dinner Mon–Fri; dinner Sat. MTR: Central. Map p 80.*

★★★ **One Harbour Road** CENTRAL *CANTONESE* There's a seemingly inexhaustible number of wonderful five-star hotel restaurants in this city of wealthy business travelers. This one stands out not only for its view of the harbor, but also for its spacious dining room, complete with a lotus pond. The food isn't creative, but it's good, with abalone, bird's nest, and roast goose all on offer. *Grand Hyatt, 1 Harbour Rd.* ☎ *852/2588-1234. Entrees $HK145–$HK250. AE, DC, MC, V. Lunch & dinner daily. MTR: Central. Map p 80.*

★★ **Peking Dumpling Wong** WAN CHAI *SHANGHAINESE* This relaxed place serves up terrific dumplings and crunchy choy sum (a green vegetable popular in Hong Kong) with oyster sauce, among other things. *Shop D/F 118 Jaffe Rd.* ☎ *852/2527-0289. Entrees $HK25–$HK128. AE, MC, V. Lunch & dinner daily. MTR: Sheung Wan. Map p 80.*

★ **Peking Garden** TSIM SHA TSUI *PEKINGESE* Peking Garden serves northern Chinese cuisine and one of the house specialties is stir-fried noodles. In fact, you can watch the staff make the noodles at 8 and 8:30 every night. *Star House, 3 Salisbury Rd.* ☎ *852/2735-8211. Entrees $HK86–$HK188. AE, DC, MC, V. Lunch & dinner daily. MTR: Tsim Sha Tsui. Map p 79.*

★★★ **Rainbow Seafood Restaurant** LAMMA *CANTONESE SEAFOOD* Of the many options in Lamma, this chain restaurant is the most reliable. It offers fresh seafood

The lobster cocktail at Spoon is not to be missed. See p 89.

served at the water's edge. A free boat takes you from Central to the restaurant and back. *Shops 1A & 1B, 16–20 1st St., Sok Kwu Wan. Entrees $HK50–$HK300. AE, DC, MC, V. Lunch & dinner daily. Ferry to Sok Kwu Wan. Map p 82.*

★★★ **Sabatini** TSIM SHA TSUI *ITALIAN* Sabatini serves Italian fare in a rustic, relaxed setting. The menu includes handmade pastas, delicious veal with morel sauce, and a huge selection of Italian wines that all go well with the evening guitar serenades. *69 Mody Rd.* ☎ *852/2733-2000. Entrees $HK250–$HK385. AE, DC, MC, V. Lunch & dinner daily. MTR: Tsim Sha Tsui. Map p 79.*

★★★ **Shui Huju** SOHO *NORTHERN CHINESE* The dark-wood interior makes this place feel more like a neighborhood spot in Beijing. The menu is superb and the clams with Chinese wine and spicy sauce, deep-fried lamb shank, and lychee wine are all standouts. *68 Peel St.* ☎ *852/2869-6927. No credit cards. Dinner daily. MTR: Central to Mid-Levels escalator. Map p 80.*

★ **Song** SOHO *VIETNAMESE* Sheathed in white, this small restaurant serves Vietnamese food at reasonable prices. The lemon-grass beef with rice vermicelli is excellent, as is the sautéed pumpkin with cashews. *75 Hollywood Rd.* ☎ *852/2559-0997. Entrees $HK150–$HK200. AE, MC, V. Lunch & dinner daily. MTR: Central to Mid-Levels escalator. Map p 80.*

★★★ Spoon by Alain Ducasse

TSIM SHA TSUI *FRENCH* This elegant spot offers a lovely view of the harbor, but you may be happily distracted by the collection of 550 hand-blown Murano glass spoons that hang from the ceiling. The French fusion menu includes steamed duck foie gras, pear and ginger chutney, and puff pastry with frogs' legs, tomato marmalade, mixed herbs, and pesto. *18 Salisbury Rd.* ☎ *852/ 2313-2323. Entrees $HK240–$HK375. AE, DC, MC, V. Dinner daily. MTR: Tsim Sha Tsui. Map p 79.*

The Square CENTRAL *CANTONESE* The big draws here are the steamed lobster dumplings and the jumbo shrimp and asparagus rolls. The dim sum menu here is rather small on the week-days, but it expands on the week-ends, so be sure to make a reservation if you plan to go then. *Exchange Square II.* ☎ *852/2525-1163. Dim sum $HK20–HK$58. AE, DC, MC, V. Lunch daily. MTR: Central. Map p 80.*

Stir-fried flour rolls with chili among the dim sum offerings at the Square.

★★ The Stoep LANTAU *SOUTH AFRICAN*

This is a favorite of mine, as there's nothing more wonderfully surreal than eating a plate of South African braai, or barbequed meat, on a laid-back beach in Hong Kong. Try a bottle of South African red wine and toss your leftovers to the roaming house dogs. *32 Lower Cheung Sha Village.* ☎ *852/2980-2699. Entrees $HK100–$HK200. AE, MC, V. Lunch & dinner daily. Central Pier,*

ferry 6 to Mui Wo. Take a cab from bus station. *Map p 82.*

★★ Super Star Seafood Restaurant

TSIM SHA TSUI *CANTONESE* Popular with the locals, there's no English menu and little atmosphere at this seafood-focused dim sum place. But pointing at pictures—or the fish or crustaceans on display in the tanks—will get you some very tasty dishes. *83–97 Nathan Rd.* ☎ *852/2628-0339. Entrees $HK70–$HK168. AE, DC, MC, V. Lunch & dinner Mon–Fri; breakfast, lunch & dinner Sat–Sun. MTR: Tsim Sha Tsui. Map p 79.*

★★ T'ang Courturant

TSIM SHA TSUI *CANTONESE* This hotel restaurant is known more for its food than its ambience (it's in a nearly windowless room). There's an English menu that clearly explains what's in each dish, and chefs who specialize in wok chi, or wok cooking at the highest achievable temperature, for tasty, sizzling results. *8 Peking Rd.* ☎ *852/ 2375-1133. Dim sum lunch $HK208. AE, DC, MC, V. Lunch daily. MTR: Tsim Sha Tsui. Map p 79.*

★ Thai Basil ADMI-

RALTY *THAI* Don't let the mall setting fool you—there's great Southeast Asian food to be had here. There are lots of excellent dishes, such as seafood *laksa* (a spicy noodle soup) and black mandarin fish filet, so order a few and share them. *Shop 005, LG/F Pacific Place, 88 Queensway.* ☎ *852/2537-4682. Entrees $HK90–$HK150. AE, DC, MC, V. Lunch & dinner daily. MTR: Admiralty. Map p 80.*

★★ 369 Shanghai Restaurant

WAN CHAI *SHANGHAINESE* This relaxed, family-run eatery has worn

Yung Kee is famous for its roast goose.

booths and chipped plates, but delicious dishes like juicy sweet and sour fish and shredded pork with green pepper make up for the lack of atmosphere. *30–32 O'Brien Rd.* ☎ *852/2527-2343. Entrees $HK40–$HK120. AE, MC, V. Lunch & dinner daily; open until 4am. MTR: Wan Chai. Map p 80.*

★★★ Tung Kee Seafood Restaurant
SAI KUNG *CANTONESE SEAFOOD* Of the many restaurants on Man Nin Street, Tung Kee has the best selection of fresh seafood, including shellfish, garoupa, and abalone. For something really different, try the lobster covered in cheese. *96–102 Man Nin St.* ☎ *852/2792-7453. Entrees $HK50–$HK300. Breakfast, lunch & dinner daily. Bus: 92 or 299. Map p 82.*

★★ Tribute
SOHO *FUSION* This tiny place takes Asian ingredients and dishes and gives them an American spin. The set menu often changes, with offerings ranging from Chinese dumplings to sea bass to hamburgers, but it's always excellent. *13 Elgin St.* ☎ *852/2135-6645. Set menu $HK398. AE, DC, MC, V. Dinner Mon–Sat. MTR: Central. Bus: 26. Map p 80.*

★★ Veda
CENTRAL *INDIAN* You'll find classic Indian dishes at this refined, elegant restaurant, alongside creative fare like tandoori lobster and Anjou pigeon with caramelized onion and mango. *8 Arbuthnot Rd.* ☎ *852/2868-5885. Entrees $HK158–$HK298. AE, DC, MC, V. Lunch & dinner daily. MTR: Central. Bus: 26. Map p 80.*

★★★ Wasabisabi
CAUSEWAY BAY *JAPANESE* With its funky interior and plethora of sushi, sashimi, and tempura choices, this place feels straight out of Tokyo. Try the *temaki* (hand-rolled sushi) and grilled salmon, which is moist and tasty. *1 Matheson St., 13th Floor.* ☎ *852/2506-0009. Entrees $HK98–$HK178. AE, DC, MC, V. Lunch & dinner daily. MTR: Causeway Bay. Map p 80.*

★★ Yellow Door Kitchen
SOHO *SICHUAN* This private restaurant is housed in a very small room reached by a rickety elevator, but the owners and staff are dedicated to offering the best Sichuan food around. The set menu changes—depending on the night; you may be treated to spicy bean curd, smoked lamb shank, or tasty Hangzhou-style duck. *37 Cochrane St. 6th Floor.* ☎ *852/2571-0913. Set menu $HK250. AE, DC, MC, V. Lunch & dinner Mon–Fri; dinner Sat. MTR: Central to Mid-Levels escalator. Map p 80.*

★★★ Yung Kee Restaurant
CENTRAL *CANTONESE* Yung Kee has been a Hong Kong institution for over 60 years thanks to its famous roast goose—which you can see hanging in the front windows. The interior has grown a little worn, but it's still got charm, and you'll get complementary dishes like preserved eggs and pickled ginger to go along with the goose. *32–40 Wellington St.* ☎ *852/2522-1624. Entrees $HK68–$HK180. AE, DC, MC, V. Lunch & dinner daily. MTR: Central. Map p 80.* ●

The Best Nightlife

Nightlife Best Bets

Best Danceable Beats
★★★ Drop, *38–43 Hollywood Rd.*
(p 100)

Best Wan Chai Bar & Dance
Floor
★★★ Klong Bar & Grill, *54–62 Lock-hart Rd. (p 98)*

Best Live Cover Bands
★★ Insomnia, *38–44 D'Augilar St.*
(p 101)

Best Place to See Models
Eating for Free
★★★ Dragon-i, *66 Wyndham St.*
(p 100)

Best Place for Absinthe
★★★ Gecko Lounge, *15–19 Holly-wood Rd. (p 101)*

Best Retro Bar
★★★ Club Feather Boa, *38 Staunton St. (p 97)*

Best Unpretentious Bar
★★ Barco, *42 Staunton St. (p 96)*

Best Place for a Drink &
a View
★★★ Aqua Spirit, *1 Peking Rd.*
(p 96)

Best Place to Throw Peanut
Shells on the Floor
★★★ Inn Side Out & East End
Brewery, *Sunning Plaza, 10 Hysan Ave. (p 97)*

Best African Bar
★★★ Makumba, *Garley Building, 48–52A Peel St. (p 98)*

Best Gay Venue
★★★ Propaganda, *1 Hollywood Rd.*
(p 100)

Best Laid-Back Dance Spot
★★ Yumla, *79 Wyndham St. (p 100)*

Best Space
★★★ 1/5, *Starcrest Building, 9 Star St. (p 100)*

Best Place to Drink on the
Street
★ Stormies, *46–50 D'Aguilar St.*
(p 99)

Many of Hong Kong's best bars have patios, where you get a ringside view of the city's nightlife.

Central Nightlife

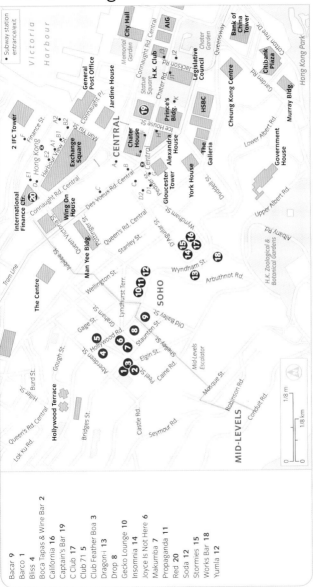

Photo p 91: Neon night in Hong Kong.

Kowloon Nightlife

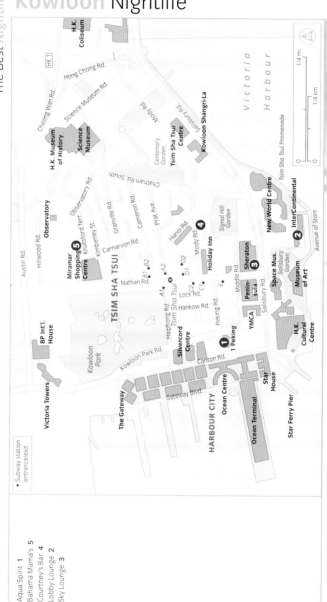

Aqua Spirit **1**
Bahama Mama's **5**
Courtney's Bar **4**
Lobby Lounge **2**
Sky Lounge **3**

Wan Chai Nightlife

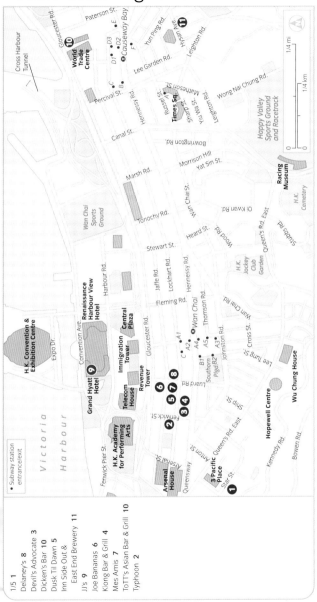

1/5 **1**
Delaney's **8**
Devil's Advocate **3**
Dicken's Bar **10**
Dusk Til Dawn **5**
Inn Side Out &
East End Brewery **11**
JJ's **9**
Joe Bananas **6**
Klong Bar & Grill **4**
Mes Amis **7**
ToTT's Asian Bar & Grill **10**
Typhoon **2**

• Subway station
  entrance/exit

Nightlife A to Z

Bars

★★★ Aqua Spirit TSIM SHA TSUI Located on the 29th floor of a high-rise, this dimly lit, sleek bar feels like a space station crossed with an art gallery. The floor-to-ceiling windows reveal the harbor and the Hong Kong skyline. When seats are available (go early or be prepared to wait) you can choose from tall stools or couches, and a creative drink list that includes the Aquatini, made of Ketel One, lychee liqueur, Chambord, and gold leaves. *1 Peking Rd.* ☎ *852/3427-2288. MTR: Tsim Sha Tsui. Map p 94.*

Bahama Mama's TSIM SHA TSUI This bar is the best option along Knutsford Terrace, which is far from the nighttime bustle of Central and Wan Chai. The scene here is still a blast, with expats and locals alike watching sports, swilling beer, and sometimes dancing on the tables. Bahama Mama's, with its Caribbean-themed decor and cheap cocktails, is a good bet for a great time. *4–5 Knutsford Terrace.* ☎ *852/2368-2121. MTR: Tsim Sha Tsui. Map p 94.*

★★ Barco SOHO This is a bar for the rest of us, with wooden stools and tables, couches in the back, and board games and magazines to pass the time. The beer and wine selection isn't vast, but it's got Carlsberg beer on tap and red wines from Australia.

The nighttime view from the elegant and romantic Aqua Spirit bar is a big draw.

Grab a spot on one of the comfortable couches and enjoy one of Captain's Bar's famous martinis.

42 Staunton St. ☎ *852/2857-4478. Bus: 13, 26, or 40M. Map p 93.*

★ California LAN KWAI FONG California has long been a fixture in the Lan Kwai Fong nightlife, and though it's now one of a plethora of options, it still can't be beat. It's a bar, club, and restaurant combined, and it's housed in a large, airy room where the prime tables have views of the street. There are televisions playing sports or music videos, as well as a live DJ who gets the dance floor going later in the evening. *24–26 Lan Kwai Fong.* ☎ *852/2521-1345. MTR: Central. Map p 93.*

★ Captain's Bar CENTRAL This dark, clubby spot where the patrons wear their work duds (albeit with ties loosened and sleeves rolled up) and smoke cigars is as close to the feel of an old British Hong Kong pub as you're likely to get. The martinis are outstanding, and beer is served in silver tankards. There's live music later in the night and a small dance floor. *Mandarin Oriental, 5 Connaught Rd.* ☎ *852/2522-0111. MTR: Central. Map p 93.*

★ China Bear LANTAU China Bear is the perfect place for a drink and a relaxing bite to eat after a day of hiking or visiting the Buddha. Choose between plastic chairs outside or the comfy booths inside, where you can catch whatever sporting event (think cricket or soccer) is showing on one of the many TVs. The waitstaff is friendly, as are many of the regulars. *Mui Wo Centre, Ngan Wan Rd.* ☎ *852/2984-7360. Ferry to Mui Wo Pier.*

★★ **Club Feather Boa** SOHO There's no sign outside the Feather Boa, but it's easy enough to find—just look for French windows covered with heavy curtains. Behind those curtains is a small, 1920s-style sitting room where the specialty is delicious frozen daiquiris. The only drawback is that the place gets packed beyond comfort after 10pm on weekends. *38 Staunton St.* ☎ *852/2857-2586. Bus: 13, 26, or 40M. Map p 93.*

★ **Club 71** CENTRAL   Tucked away on a tree-lined alley, this is a mellow bar where patrons play board games outside when the weather is nice and inside at the long bar when it's too hot to be far from air-conditioning. *67 Hollywood Rd.* ☎ *852/2858-7071. Bus: 26. Map p 93.*

★★ **Courtney's Bar** TSIM SHA TSUI   This lounge, located in the hip boutique hotel The Minden, is named after local artist Pauline Courtney, whose Sri-Lankan/Australian/Hong Kong–influenced paintings adorn the walls. There's an outdoor terrace that extends the space, and snacks are served in the early evening (as is breakfast in the morning). *7 Minden Ave.* ☎ *852-2729-7777. MTR: Tsim Sha Tsui. Map p 94.*

★★ **Delaney's** WAN CHAI   It has been said more than once (especially after a few pints) that there is at least one good Irish pub in every major city in the world. In Hong Kong, that pub is Delaney's. With two large floors and many TVs, you can be sure to get a Guinness and a game here. *18 Luard Rd.* ☎ *852/2804-2880. Map p 95.*

★★ **Devil's Advocate** WAN CHAI This spot is notable for being a surprisingly unpretentious sports bar in the heart of Wan Chai. With huge booths, a long bar, and tables near the street, it's a good place to hit for happy hour, when drinks are two for one. *48–50 Lockhart Rd.* ☎ *852/ 2865-7271. MTR: Wan Chai. Map p 95.*

★ **Dicken's Bar** CAUSEWAY BAY A sprawling bar with loads of tables, multiple TVs, and pub food served until 11pm. Soccer fans often come here to watch games, and the staff is friendly. Prices are a bit high, but it's a relaxing atmosphere after a day of shopping in Causeway Bay. *281 Gloucester Rd.* ☎ *852/2837-6782. MTR: Causeway Bay. Map p 95.*

★ **Diesel Sports Bar** LAMMA If you don't mind a little grit (mostly sand from the beach), this is an entertaining spot to catch soccer and rugby matches on the numerous TVs. The bartenders are welcoming and the crowd is made up mainly of expats who live on the island. *51 Main St., Yung Shue Wan.* ☎ *852/2982-4116. Ferry to Lamma.*

★★★ **Inn Side Out & East End Brewery** CAUSEWAY BAY   These two bars, connected by an outdoor patio filled with tables, have the best

Patrons at Inn Side Out enjoy the outdoor seating.

international selection of beer in Hong Kong, great service, and, best of all, you're encouraged to throw the shells from the complimentary peanuts on the ground. Start the night here and see if you can pull yourself away. *Sunning Plaza, 10 Hysan Ave.* ☎ *852/2895-2900. MTR: Causeway Bay. Map p 95.*

★★ **JJ's** WAN CHAI The two-story JJ's was redesigned in 2006 into an elegant bar with private tables hidden in corners. The Music Room upstairs has classic record covers on the walls and a large stage for JJ's house band to play R&B standards and other covers in the evenings. *Grand Hyatt, 1 Harbour Rd.* ☎ *852/2529-1811. MTR: Wan Chai. Map p 95.*

★ **Joe Bananas** WAN CHAI Joe Bananas is one of Hong Kong's oldest bars, and over the years it has transformed from a place where men picked up women of ill repute to a place where both men and women try to pick up each other. It has a spacious dance floor and tables near the street. *23 Luard Rd.* ☎ *852/2529-1811. MTR: Wan Chai. Map p 95.*

The patio at Red offers fantastic views of the city.

Enjoy the pub fare and the water views at the Pickled Pelican.

★★ **Joyce Is Not Here** SOHO Joyce bills her bar as an artists' haven, and holds poetry readings and movie screenings throughout the week. The place is small and a bit cluttered with paintings, books, and even mannequins dressed in hats and boas. The crowd is bohemian and nearly banker free. *38–44 Peel St.* ☎ *852/2851-2999. Bus: 13, 26, or 40M. Map p 93.*

★★★ **Klong Bar & Grill** WAN CHAI The downstairs of this Thai-themed bar and grill looks like a narrow hallway with tables along the sides. Upstairs is a more luxurious affair—private tables, a U-shaped bar, a DJ, and a dance floor that gets more crowded as the night rolls on. *54–62 Lockhart Rd.* ☎ *852/2217-8330. MTR: Wan Chai. Map p 95.*

★★ **Lobby Lounge** TSIM SHA TSUI This sea of tables and booths is located behind the check-in desk at the Intercontinental, but that doesn't detract from its amazing view of Hong Kong Island, comfortable seating, and chilled out live music in the evenings. *18 Salisbury Rd.* ☎ *852/2721-1211. MTR: Tsim Sha Tsui. Map p 94.*

★★★ **Makumba** CENTRAL A basement bar that is decked out with furniture and art from Africa, Makumba hosts a DJ or live music on the weekends, often playing African tunes or reggae. *Garley Building, 48–52A Peel St.* ☎ *852/ 2834-6366. MTR: Central. Bus: 13, 26, or 40M. Map p 93.*

★ **Pickled Pelican** STANLEY   This British-style pub has a large selection of whiskey and sports on the TVs around the bar. Although there's a crush of options on the waterfront in Stanley, this bar is notable for its excellent service and better-than-average pub food, like the potato fish cakes and garden salad. *90 Stanley Main St.* ☎ *852/2868-6026. Bus: 6, 6X, 6A, 260, or 973.*

Red CENTRAL   This hip bar on the fourth floor of the IFC mall offers an outdoor patio with panoramic views of Victoria Harbour and the skyline. You can order healthy California cuisine while watching the lights come on in the Central skyscrapers. There is live jazz on Thursday nights starting at 10pm. *IFC mall, 8 Finance St.* ☎ *852/8129-8882. MTR: Central. Map p 93.*

★★ **Sky Lounge** TSIM SHA TSUI Plush and elegant, this bar at the top of the Sheraton combines great views and quality cocktails. It's pricey, but you get what you pay for in terms of the service and the scenery—there's a view from almost every seat. *20 Nathan Rd.*

Revelers take to the streets during a typical night out in Lan Kwai Fong.

☎ *852/2369-1111. MTR: Tsim Sha Tsui. Map p 94.*

★★ **Soda** CENTRAL   The location of this bar is terrific—it's smack in between Lan Kwai Fong (LKF) and SoHo. The atmosphere is both trendy and relaxed, with colorful lighting and TVs behind the bar. The location tends to make it a transit point throughout the night, but it's worth getting a drink here before moving on to rowdy LKF or more chilled-out SoHo spots. *79 Wyndham St.* ☎ *852/ 2522-8118. Bus: 26. Map p 93.*

★ **Stormies** LAN KWAI FONG On a weekend night, it's easy to find Stormies: Just look for the hordes of people holding plastic cups on the

Happy hour at Dusk til Dawn runs from 5 to 11pm, and draws a mostly expat crowd.

The Dragon-i is one of Hong Kong's most talked about clubs, thanks in part to its model clientele.

street outside. The interior is huge, with two floors and plenty of seating, but the best way to enjoy this place is to take a drink out onto the street with the masses. *46–50 D'Aguilar St.* ☎ *852/2845-5533. MTR: Central. Map p 93.*

★ **Typhoon** WAN CHAI   Typhoon is a chic newcomer to Wan Chai, with a stylish round bar and a huge TV screen for sporting events. Even when it's packed, it's less raucous than many other options in this part of the city, though the music can be very loud. *37–39 Lockhart Rd.* ☎ *852/2527-2077. MTR: Wan Chai. Map p 95.*

Clubs

★ **C Club** LAN KWAI FONG   Located in the heart of Lan Kwai Fong, this basement club attracts a younger crowd. There is a bar and some booths at the front, with the dance floor in the back and a DJ who generally plays mainstream hip-hop. *9–11 Lan Kwai Fong.* ☎ *852/2186-1897. MTR: Central. Map p 93.*

★★★ **Dragon-i** CENTRAL   A restaurant, bar, and dance club in one, Dragon-i has long been a hot spot in Hong Kong. In fact, the tables surrounding the dance floor are often occupied by models, who are invited to eat here for free. Getting past the doorman can be a challenge, but dressing well and chatting him up

may yield success. *The Centrium, 60 Wyndham St.* ☎ *852/3110-1222. MTR: Central. Bus: 26. Map p 93.*

★★★ **Drop** CENTRAL   Located down a narrow alley, this club has a square bar flanking a dance floor, couches, and a high-rise stage for the DJ. The music is usually very deep and funky, and there are some cozy tables in the back that are easier to commandeer if you arrive early. *38–43 Hollywood Rd.* ☎ *852/ 2543-8856. MTR: Central. Bus: 26. Map p 93.*

★★★ **1/5** WAN CHAI   This is one of my favorite spaces in Hong Kong, as it's both elegant and comfortable, with a dance floor near the entrance and tables and couches tucked in the back. The music can be hit or miss, but it's always danceable. *Starcrest Building, 9 Star St.* ☎ *852/2520-2515. MTR: Admiralty. Map p 95.*

★★ **Yumla** CENTRAL   A small, somewhat gritty looking club, Yumla offers terrific music in a laid-back, welcoming atmosphere. The bar is sometimes hard to reach across the packed dance floor, so be patient. *79 Wyndham St.* ☎ *852/2147-2383. MTR: Central. Bus: 26. Map p 93.*

Gay Clubs & Bars

★ **Bliss** SOHO   Split between two levels, this stylish spot has two bars, including a lounge that is a bit less hectic than the dance floor. The crowd here dresses to kill, but that doesn't mean you have to. *1 Elgin St.* ☎ *852/3110-1222. MTR: Central. Bus: 13, 26, or 40M. Map p 93.*

★★★ **Propaganda** CENTRAL   This is Hong Kong's best-known gay club, with a massive dance floor, a wide drink selection, and a balcony perfect for watching the crowd below. It's popular among tourists even though it's a bit hard to find (*Hint:* it's in the alley off Pottinger

Night Touring

Not in the mood for bar hopping? Take a tour of the harbor and see the glittering lights of Hong Kong in all their glory. **The Aberdeen & Harbour Night Cruise** takes you on a nearly 5-hour ride, which includes drinks and dinner. Go to www.watertours.com.hk for information, or call ☎ 852/2926-3868. Tour companies like **Gray Line** (☎ 852/2368-7111; www.grayline.com.hk), and **Splendid Tours & Travel** (☎ 852/2316-2151; www.splendidtours.com) also offer night tours of the city—you'll get a sense of what Hong Kong is really like after the sun goes down.

St.). *1 Hollywood Rd.* ☎ *852/2868-1316. MTR: Central. Bus: 13, 26, or 40M. Map p 93.*

★ **Works Bar** CENTRAL Works shares the same owner as Propaganda, and is sometimes more crowded on the weekend. It also has a huge dance floor and plenty of drink options, but it's a bit easier to find. It also tends to have a more mixed crowd. *30–32 Wyndham St.* ☎ *852/2868-6102. MTR: Central. Bus: 13, 26, or 40M. Map p 93.*

Live Music

★★ **Dusk til Dawn** WAN CHAI This spot has seating along the edges of the room and at the bar, with a dance floor in the center with a stage for live acts. They book some very good cover bands, playing mostly American rock. The place stays open late, but the crowd can get a little less appealing as the night winds down, so plan to come on the early side. *76–84 Jaffe Rd.* ☎ *852/2528-4689. MTR: Wan Chai. Map p 95.*

★★★ **Gecko Lounge** CENTRAL Owned by a bespectacled, lovable Frenchman, this lounge hosts live jazz Tuesday to Thursday. It's a reclusive setting with comfortable couches lining the walls and they even serve absinthe. In other words, it's perfect

for a romantic night out. *15–19 Hollywood Rd.* ☎ *852/2537-4680. MTR: Central. Bus: 26. Map p 93.*

★★ **Insomnia** LAN KWAI FONG Come early to this live music venue in the center of Lan Kwai Fong and you may be lucky enough to nab a seat at the bar, which is open to the street. The bands (mostly cover bands playing Western hits) is in the back and the dance floor can get very crowded as the night wears on. *38–44 D'Aguilar St.* ☎ *852/2525-0957. Daily 8pm–6am. MTR: Central. Map p 93.*

★ **ToTT's Asian Bar & Grill** CAUSEWAY BAY This is a fun, if slightly tacky bar—the seating is upholstered in zebra stripes—at the

Many bars and nightclubs in Hong Kong have dance floors, and DJs get the crowds moving.

top of the Excelsior Hotel. The views of the harbor are terrific, and the large selection of cocktails, including quality martinis and a variety of international wines, is complemented by the live bands who play later in the evening. *281 Gloucester Rd.* ☎ *852/2837-6786. MTR: Causeway Bay. Map p 95.*

Wine Bars

★ **Bacar** SOHO   Though a bit cramped, this wine bar is stylish, and has a massive selection of wine by the glass. Try their Australian reds for a taste of the best the Asia-Pacific region has to offer. *22 Shelley St.* ☎ *852/2521-8325. Bus: 13, 26, or 40M. Map p 93.*

★★ **Boca Tapas & Wine Bar** SOHO   This candlelit Spanish-themed bar is dark and moody in the best possible way. The wine selection is good, with the best offerings from Spain. It's a bit pricey, but the pours are generous and the tapas is excellent. *65 Peel St.* ☎ *852/2548-1717. Bus: 13, 26, or 40M. Map p 93.*

Try the absinthe at Gecko Lounge. See p 101.

★★ **Mes Amis** WAN CHAI   This bar/restaurant/club is a big, open space with plenty of tables that get moved to make way for a dance floor when the DJ starts spinning. There's a large wine selection, and snacks like nachos and quesadillas. The extra-long happy hour (it runs 4–9pm) draws the working crowd. *83 Lockhart Rd.* ☎ *852/2527-6680. MTR: Wan Chai. Map p 95.*

From Cheesy to Sleazy

Nightlife in Hong Kong varies by widely by neighborhood, and in a city this walkable and this packed with bars and clubs, it's fun to pick an area to explore, rather than picking one spot at which to spend your evening. Here's a quick look at to what to expect when you hit the town in a few of Hong Kong's neighborhoods.

Lan Kwai Fong: Loud and crowded, this area is aimed at 20-somethings looking for a party, though plenty of 40-somethings seem to enjoy it as well.

Mongkok: If you want a true taste of Chinese Hong Kong nightlife, try any of Mongkok's small local bars, where the beer is served in buckets and the karoake is deafening.

Soho: If you want a slightly higher-end party scene, skip LKF and head to Soho.

Tsim Sha Tsui: Knutsford Terrace offers the best place to find outdoor seating for a late night drink.

Wan Chai: This area can get a bit seedy, so head to Star Street, where there are quaint, hip restaurants and bars.

Arts & Entertainment
Best Bets

Best Place to Spend an Afternoon with the Kids
★★ Ocean Park, *Ocean Park Rd.* (p 107)

Best Movie Theater
★★★ Broadway Cinematheque Prosperous Garden, *3 Public Sq.* (p 108)

Best Horse Racing Track
★★★ Sha Tin Racecourse, *Sha Tin* (p 110)

Best Tapas & Live Music
★★ Bohemian Lounge, *3–5 Bailey St.* (p 111)

Best Place to Learn a Karate Chop
★★ Kung Fu Corner, *22 Austin Rd.* (p 113)

Best Boat Ride
★★★ Duk Ling Ride, *Kowloon Public Pier* (p 107)

Best New Orleans Jazz
★★ Ned Kelly's Last Stand, *11A Ashley Rd.* (p 111)

Best Dancers
★★★ Hong Kong Ballet, Hong Kong Cultural Centre, *10 Salisbury Rd.* (p 110)

Best Place to Recite Poetry
★★★ Fringe Club, *2 Lower Albert Rd.* (p 113)

Best Public Golf Course
★★★ Jockey Club Kau Sai Chau Public Golf Course, *Kau Sai Chau*

Best Massage
★★★ Chuan Spa, Langham Place Hotel, *555 Shanghai St., 41st floor* (p 112)

Best Nighttime Horse Races
★★★ Happy Valley Racecourse, *2 Sports Rd.* (p 110)

Best Place for Kung Fu Movies
★★ Film Archive Cinema, *50 Lei King Rd.* (p 108)

Best Cantonese Opera
★★★ Hong Kong City Hall, *5 Edinburgh Place* (p 109)

Horses come out of the gate at Happy Valley Racecourse, where both locals and visitors put money on the races.

Kowloon A&E

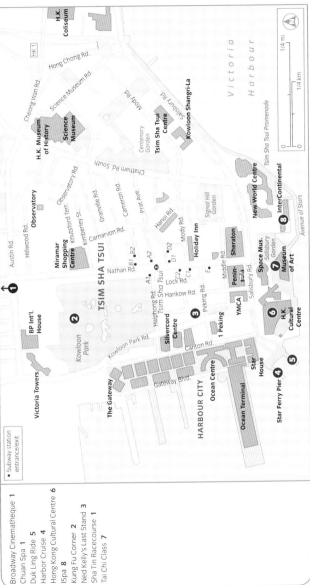

Broadway Cinematheque 1
Chuan Spa 1
Duk Ling Ride 5
Harbor Cruise 4
Hong Kong Cultural Centre 6
iSpa 8
Kung Fu Corner 2
Ned Kelly's Last Stand 3
Sha Tin Racecourse 1
Tai Chi Class 7

Photo p 103: A dancer with the Hong Kong Ballet.

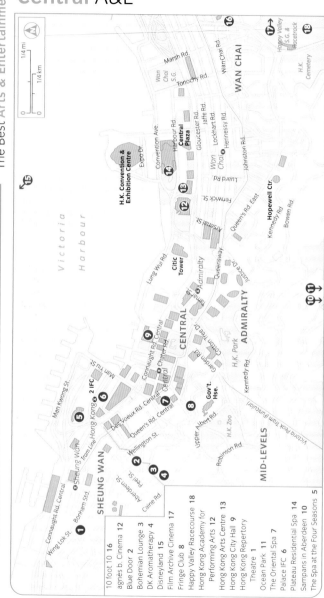

Victoria Harbour

SHEUNG WAN

CENTRAL

ADMIRALTY

MID-LEVELS

WAN CHAI

H.K. Convention & Exhibition Centre

Central Plaza

Citic Tower

Gov't. Hse.

Hopewell Ctr.

Happy Valley

1/4 mi
1/4 km

Arts & Entertainment A to Z

Amusement Parks

★ kids Hong Kong Disneyland

LANTAU   The press skewered Disneyland when it opened here (in 2005) for being too small, but there's enough here to keep you busy for at least part of a day. Most of the attractions are Disney standards, like Main Street U.S.A., Fantasyland, and Tomorrowland. The one innovation is the world's only Fantasy Gardens where Mickey, Minnie, and the rest of the crew mingle with visitors. In addition, there are rides (like Space Mountain), parades, and shows. Be aware that admission prices go up during peak times, like summer vacation (July/Aug) and public holidays. ☎ 852/1-830-830. www.park. hongkongdisneyland.com. Admission $HK295 adults; $HK210 kids 3–11. MTR: Disneyland stop. Map p 106.

★★ kids Ocean Park ABERDEEN

This amusement park and marine center have something for everyone. Small wonder, then, that Ocean Park is a local favorite. It features rides including a "turbo drop," which sends thrill seekers into free fall for 5 seconds; a roller coaster called the Dragon; and a large Ferris wheel. There are also marine and bird exhibits, a butterfly walk, and daily performances by the park's seals and dolphins. Ocean Park Rd. ☎ 852/ 2552-0291. www.oceanpark.com.hk. Admission $HK185 adults; $HK93 kids 3–11. Bus: 6A, 6X, 70, 75, 90, 97, or 260. Map p 106.

Boat Rides

★★ kids Dolphinwatch Cruise

TSIM SHA TSUI   Hong Kong's pink dolphins are local celebrities—not surprising, given their flamingo tint and the fact that they're not found anywhere else in the world. They're also a threatened species thanks to pleasure boaters and pollution. Dolphinwatch runs responsible trips to see these cool creatures in the waters around Lantau. Take advantage while you still can. ☎ 852/2984-1414. www.hkdolphinwatch.com. Tickets $HK360 adults; $HK180 kids under 12. Pickup from various hotels.

★★★ Duk Ling Ride TSIM SHA

TSUI   Every so often, an apparently ancient Chinese junk goes puttering through Victoria Harbour amid the

Mickey Mouse wears a traditional Chinese outfit for a parade at Hong Kong Disneyland.

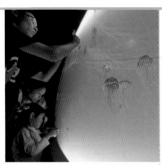

Visitors can get an up-close look at jellyfish and other marine creatures at Ocean Park. See p 107.

high-speed ferries and container ships. It's the *Duk Ling,* a modern boat designed to look like the junks that dominated Hong Kong's waters hundreds of years ago. The ride is free, and on a clear day, you'll get great views. *Kowloon Public Pier (to the left of the Star Ferry Pier).* ☎ *852/ 2508-1234. www.dukling.com.hk. MTR: Tsim Sha Tsui. Map p 105.*

★★ **Harbor Cruise** TSIM SHA TSUI   You can take either a 30-minute or a 2-hour cruise in the evenings, when buildings on both sides of the harbor participate in a laser-and-light show. The show isn't so spectacular if it's hazy, so wait for a clear night. *Tsim Sha Tsui Star Ferry Pier.* ☎ *852/2118-6201. www.discoverhongkong.com. Tickets $HK120 30-min cruise; $HK290 2-hr. cruise. MTR: Tsim Sha Tsui Star Ferry Pier. Map p 105.*

★★ **Sampans in Aberdeen** ABERDEEN   On the pier just across the street from the bus station in Aberdeen, you can hire *sampans,* traditional Chinese fishing boats, for a short spin. The harbor here was once home to fishing families, people who were born, raised, and died living on their boats. These days, development has changed the life of this community, but you can still see a few of these family boats out in the water. *Aberdeen Promenade, south of Aberdeen Praya Rd. Price is negotiable, around HK$50 for a short trip. Bus: 70, 73, or 973. Map p 106.*

Cinema

★★ **agnès b. Cinema** WAN CHAI   This movie theater screens independent films, classics, and revivals. agnès b. celebrates Hong Kong's vibrant filmmaking tradition, and the Hong Kong film festival is held here every summer. *Hong Kong*

Don't miss a chance to see Hong Kong's endangered pink dolphins. See p 107.

A sign outside a Cantonese opera performance explains who is playing each character.

Arts Centre, 2 Harbour Rd. ☎ 852/2582-0200. www.hkac.org.hk. Admission $HK50. MTR: Wan Chai. Map p 106.

★★★ **Broadway Cinematheque**
YAU MA TEI   Showing international mainstream films and art-house hits, this theater is my favorite spot for a night at the movies. There's a lobby shop selling posters and postcards and a bookshop/cafe that offers English-language books on film and other topics. *Prosperous Garden, 3 Public Sq.* ☎ *852/2388-3188. www.cinema.com.hk. Tickets $HK80. MTR: Yau Ma Tei. Map p 105.*

★★ **Film Archive Cinema** SAI WAN HO   This archive is a great resource for those who want to delve into Hong Kong filmmaking, past and present. On any given night, you'll see films like the 1959 Cantonese Opera movie, *The Purple Hairpin,* or kung fu epics like *Sacred Fire, Heroic Wind* from 1966. *50 Lei King Rd.* ☎ *852/2739-2139. www.filmarchive.gov.hk. MTR: Sai Wan Ho. Map p 106.*

★ **Palace IFC** CENTRAL   The Palace is my favorite place to catch mainstream, Western films. If you get popcorn, ask for a mix of sweet and salty. *IFC Mall, 8 Finance St.* ☎ *852/2388-6268. www.ifc.com.hk/english/cinema.aspx. Tickets $HK40–$HK70. MTR: Central. Map p 106.*

Dance, Opera, & Classical Music

★★ **Cantonese Opera** CENTRAL
It's not uncommon to stumble upon a Cantonese opera performance just by chance—look for elaborately decorated canopies held up by bamboo scaffolding—since the city stages free public performances. But you can also buy tickets to shows at venues like Hong Kong's City Hall (see "Hong Kong City Hall," below). Though the operas are, of course, in Cantonese, you'll usually be handed a summary of the plot so you can follow along.

★ **Hong Kong Academy for Performing Arts** WAN CHAI
This funky glass building in the heart of Hong Kong is both a school

The Duk Ling, a traditional Chinese junk, sails through Victoria Harbour.

and a hot spot for art, theater, and music. Though not everything here is polished or professional, you'll see emerging local and international artists at work. *1 Gloucester Rd.* ☎ *852/2584-8500. www.hkapa. edu. Tickets $HK80 and up. MTR: Wan Chai. Bus: 18. Map p 106.*

★★ Hong Kong City Hall CEN-TRAL

This harbor-side venue has a constant stream of shows, from theater to dance and jazz. Check the website for listings or just drop by to see what's on. *5 Edinburgh Place* ☎ *852/2921-2840. www.cityhall. gov.hk. Tickets $HK100 and up. MTR: Central. Map p 106.*

★★★ Hong Kong Cultural Centre WAN CHAI

With its wing-shaped, beige exterior, it may seem surprising that this is Hong Kong's most active venue for classical music, dance, opera, and other major cultural performances. You'll see the Hong Kong Philharmonic here, as well as the Hong Kong Chinese Orchestra and Hong Kong Ballet. *10 Salisbury Rd.* ☎ *852/2734-2009. www.hkculturalcentre.gov.hk. Tickets $HK100 and up. MTR: Tsim Sha Tsui. Map p 105.*

Horse Racing

★★★ Happy Valley Racecourse HAPPY VALLEY

Happy Valley is one of the few in-city racecourses in the world. With its views of the surrounding skyscrapers and its electrified atmosphere, it's worth a visit whether or not you put money on the outcome. Races are generally held on Wednesday nights. Dining options range from hamburgers to dim sum, and beer is available on tap. The track shuts down for most of July and all of August. *2 Sports Rd.* ☎ *852/2895-1523. www.happy valleyracecourse.com. Admission $HK10. MTR: Causeway Bay. Bus: 75, 90, or 97. Map p 106.*

★★★ Sha Tin Racecourse SHA TIN

I'll confess: I actually prefer this place to Happy Valley. It's not as glitzy, but it draws a mostly local crowd to watch the horses run on Saturdays, and more attention is paid to the races and less to socializing. There are abundant Cantonese and Western fast-food options. *Sha Tin Racecourse.* ☎ *852/2695-6223. www.sha-tin.com. Tickets $HK10. KCR: Sha Tin Racecourse. Map p 105.*

I've Got a Horse Right Here

Although there are only two horse racing tracks in Hong Kong, you can see racing's presence all over the city thanks to the blue Hong Kong Jockey Club betting points. On Wednesdays and Saturdays, you may also notice certain Hong Kong locals (mostly older men) going about their business while carrying both a radio and a marked-up newspaper—a sure sign they've got money on the races. Hong Kong's Happy Valley Racecourse was founded by the British in 1846, and the Sha Tin course opened in 1978. Both are run by the Hong Kong Jockey Club, which makes a killing (but also gives a lot to local charity). Horse racing is technically the only form of legal gambling in Hong Kong, though people often make bets on mahjong, card games, and liar's dice.

A jazz guitarist performs at Blue Door, one of the best places to hear live jazz in Hong Kong.

Live Music

★★★ **Blue Door** CENTRAL   Good jazz can be hard to find in Asia, but this small venue off the Mid-Levels escalator often surprises with strong international and local acts. The setting is intimate and dark, with tables and chairs clustered together in a narrow space. *Cheung Hing Commercial Building, 37 Cochrane St., 5th Floor,* ☎ *852/2858-6555. www.bluedoor.com.hk. Bus 13, 26, or 40M. Map p 106.*

★★ **Bohemian Lounge** SOHO This bar, just up from Hollywood Road, has a plush interior and live music (mostly jazz) at the end of the week and on weekends. The drink selection is broad and reasonably priced, and if you want to have a conversation while the music is on, you can usually find a quieter table in the back. They also serve decent tapas. *3–5 Old Bailey St.* ☎ *852/2526-6099. Bus: 13, 26, or 40M. Map p 106.*

★★ **Ned Kelly's Last Stand** TSIM SHA TSUI   The bands at this dark-wood bar mostly play New Orleans jazz—great stuff, but not so

conducive to conversation. The beer selection here is excellent, and the service is fast and friendly. *11A Ashley Rd.* ☎ *852/2376-0562. MTR: Tsim Sha Tsui. Map p 105.*

The feng shui–inspired decor at the Chuan Spa.

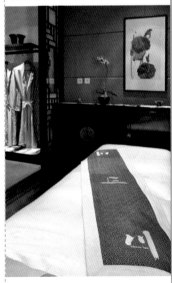

The Best Arts & Entertainment

Spas & Foot Massages

★★ 10 foot 10 CAUSEWAY BAY

This small acupuncture and foot reflexology shop stands out for its high quality treatments and helpful staff. Practitioners of foot reflexology believe they can cure or prevent illness by applying pressure to specific points on the feet. Whether or not they're right, their technique certainly feels good. Stop in and give your toes a real Hong Kong treat. *Bartlock Centre, 3 Yiu Wa St, 2nd floor.* ☎ *852/2591-9188. Prices start at \$HK118 for 30 min. foot reflexology treatment. www.10-foot-10.com. MTR: Causeway Bay. Map p 106.*

★★★ Chuan Spa MONGKOK

Located in the beautiful Langham Place Hotel, this spa is an oasis of calm, with private, pre-treatment tearooms and decor that evokes the five elements of feng shui—fire, earth, water, wood, and metal. They offer everything from massages and facials to a combination package called the Tao of Detox (\$HK1,645). *Langham Place Hotel, 555 Shanghai St, 41st floor.* ☎ *852/3552-3388. Prices start at \$HK550 for facials;* \$HK795 for a 1-hour massage. www. chuanspa.com/en. MTR: Mongkok. Map 105.

DK Aromatherapy SOHO

This bright, modern spa specializes in aromatherapy, but you can also get a massage or other treatments while you're here. DK Aromatherapy even offers an "Animal Communications Workshop" where you'll learn how to commune with your pets. The price is \$HK1,100 and you're asked to bring a photo of your furry loved one. *16A Staunton St.* ☎ *852/2771-2847. www.aroma.com.hk. Treatments \$HK380 and up. Bus: 12, 13, 26. Map 106.*

★★ I Spa TSIM SHA TSUI

Not surprisingly, most of Hong Kong's four-star hotels offer spas. The difference here, at the InterContinental's in-house spa, is that some treatment rooms have views of the harbor and the skyline. I can't say I've tried it, but the Beauty Tox treatment (prices start at \$HK1,100) is reputed to have a 'botox-effect' without the use of needles. Or you could just relax and enjoy the sauna. *InterContinental Hotel, 18 Salisbury Rd, 3rd floor.* ☎ *852/2721-1211. Prices vary based*

The spa at the Four Seasons offers serious luxury and excellent skyline views.

on treatment. www.hongkong-ic. intercontinental.com. MTR: Tsim Sha Tsui. Map 105.

★★ The Oriental Spa CENTRAL

This four-star spa has got it all, from traditional Chinese medicine to Swedish massages. They even offer a Chinese Herbal Steam Room. The facilities are strikingly elegant, and incredibly relaxing, with Chinese art and marble interiors throughout. There is also an old-fashioned barbershop where men can get a shave and a haircut. *Landmark Mandarin Oriental, 15 Queen's Rd, 5th and 6th floors,* ☎ *852/2132-0011. Prices vary based on treatment. www.mandarin oriental.com/hotel/556000004.asp. MTR: Central. Map 106.*

★★ Plateau Residential Spa

CENTRAL   This spa not only has a huge list of options and great service, but if you're a guest you can also use the Grand Hyatt's other offerings, such as the outdoor pool and grill restaurant. Treatments include combinations of Swedish massage, Thai massage, and hot stone therapy, in which hot stones are rubbed against the body. *Grand Hyatt Hotel, 1 Harbour Rd, 11th floor.* ☎ *852/2584-7688. Prices vary based on treatment. www.plateau.com.hk. MTR: Wan Chai. Map 106.*

★★ The Spa at the Four Seasons CENTRAL   This four-star spa offers two spa suites where you can spend the night, and 18 spa rooms with earth tone designs that use stone and glass materials to make for a relaxed atmosphere. Many rooms have excellent views of the harbor, visible while you're getting your massage. *The Four Seasons Hotel, 8 Finance St.* ☎ *852/3196-8888. Prices vary based on treatment. www.fourseasons.com. MTR: Central. Map 106.*

The Fringe Club occupies a former dairy-farm depot built in 1813, and it hosts many English-language acts. See p 114.

Sports & Activities

★★ Kung Fu Corner TSIM SHA TSUI   Every Sunday in Kowloon Park, the Hong Kong Tourism Board puts on a traditional kung fu demonstration. The event includes drumming and dragon dancing (that's when two or more people cover themselves with a cloth dragon and dance in unison). After the show, those brave enough can learn a few moves. *22 Austin Rd.* ☎ *852/2724-3344. www. discoverhongkong.com. MTR: Tsim Sha Tsui. Map p 105.*

★★ Tai Chi Class TSIM SHA TSUI

Practitioners of tai chi believe it keeps the body fit and the mind relaxed and focused. Technically a form of martial arts, tai chi is really a slow, deliberate exercise—you'll see people performing it in parks all over the city. Thanks to the Hong Kong Tourism Board, Mr. Ng, a tai chi master, gives free beginner's classes several days a week. Call in advance to book a spot. *Sculpture Court, Museum of Art.* ☎ *852/2508-1234. www.discover hongkong.com. MTR: Tsim Sha Tsui. Map p 105.*

Theater
★★★ Fringe Club CENTRAL This is one of the best venues in Hong Kong for seeing contemporary theater, live music, and poetry readings. Some of the acts are international, but many are local performers and writers. There's also a rooftop bar and the restaurant M at the Fringe offers excellent pre- or post-show dining. *2 Lower Albert Rd.* ☎ *852/2521-7251. www.hkfringe club.com. Tickets $HK100 and up. MTR: Central. Map p 106.*

★★ Hong Kong Arts Centre
WAN CHAI You can catch plays and other performances, mostly by local groups, at this arts center, which also houses galleries and a movie theater. *2 Harbour Rd.* ☎ *852/2582-0200. www.hkac.org.hk. Tickets $HK80 and up. MTR: Wan Chai. Bus: 18. Map p 106.*

★★ Hong Kong Repertory Theatre
CENTRAL The troupe here puts on both original works and established classics from China and elsewhere. The venue feels slightly industrial, with seats crammed together, but the shows are worth it. *Sheung Wan Municipal Services Building, 345 Queen's Rd., 4th Floor.* ☎ *852/3103-5930. www. hkrep.com. MTR: Sheung Wan. Map p 106.* ●

The Hong Kong Cultural Centre is the home of many of the city's best known performing arts groups. See p 109.

9 The Best **Lodging**

Lodging Best Bets

Best **Historic Hotel**
★★★ Peninsula Hotel $$$$
Salisbury Rd. (p 126)

Best **Luxury Hotel**
★★★ Four Seasons $$$$
8 Finance St. (p 121)

Best **Outdoor Pool**
★★★ Grand Hyatt $$$ *1 Harbour Rd.*
(p 122)

Best **Spa Rooms**
★★★ Langham Place Hotel $$$$
555 Shanghai St. (p 125)

Best **Old World Library**
★★★ Island Shangri-La $$$$
Pacific Place, Supreme Court Rd.
(p 123)

Best **at the Airport**
Regal Airport Hotel $$$ *9 Cheong*
Tat Rd. (p 126)

Most **Helpful Staff**
★★ The Excelsior $$ *281 Glouces-*
ter Rd. (p 121)

Best **Place to Hike to**
Sunset Peak
★ Hong Kong Bank Foundation
SG David Hostel $ *Ngong Ping*
(p 123)

Best **Rooftop Tennis Court**
★★ The Excelsior $$ *281 Glouces-*
ter Rd. (p 121)

Best **Boutique Hotel**
★★ JIA Boutique Hotel $$
1–5 Irving St. (p 123)

Best **Harbor-View Rooms**
★★★ InterContinental Hong Kong
$$$$ *18 Salisbury Rd. (p 123)*

Best **East Meets West**
★★★ Mandarin Oriental $$$$
5 Connaught Rd. (p 125)

Best **Bar-Hopping Location**
★ Hotel LKF $$ *33 Wyndham St.*
(p 123)

Best **Value**
★ The Salisbury YMCA $
41 Salisbury Rd. (p 127)

Most **Spacious Rooms**
★★★ Landmark Mandarin Oriental
$$$$ *15 Queen's Rd. (p 124)*

Best **Bathrooms**
★★★ Langham Hotel $$$$ *8*
Peking Rd. (p 124)

Most **Kid Friendly**
★★★ The Ritz-Carlton $$$$
3 Connaught Rd. (p.127)

Rooms at the Landmark Mandarin Oriental are now bigger thanks to renovations in 2006.

Kowloon Lodging

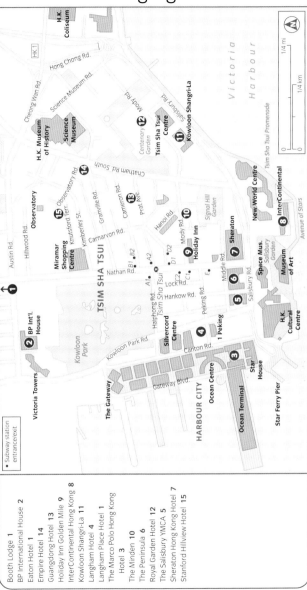

Booth Lodge **1**
BP International House **2**
Eaton Hotel **1**
Empire Hotel **14**
Guangdong Hotel **13**
Holiday Inn Golden Mile **9**
InterContinental Hong Kong **8**
Kowloon Shangri-La **11**
Langham Hotel **4**
Langham Place Hotel **1**
The Marco Polo Hong Kong Hotel **3**
The Minden **10**
The Peninsula **6**
Royal Garden Hotel **12**
The Salisbury YMCA **5**
Sheraton Hong Kong Hotel **7**
Stanford Hillview Hotel **15**

Photo p 115: A room at the InterContinental.

The Best Lodging

Central Lodging

JW Marriott Hong Kong **11**
Landmark Mandarin Oriental **6**
Mandarin Oriental **7**
Metropark Hotel **20**
The Park Lane **17**

Regal Airport Hotel **2**
Renaissance Harbour View
  Hotel **14**
The Ritz-Carlton **8**
Rosedale on the Park **19**

Lodging A to Z

Alisan Guest House CAUSEWAY BAY   The rooms here may be sparsely furnished, but they're clean and the place has many other pluses. The English-speaking manager offers great advice for getting around Hong Kong. This spot also has some of the cheapest rates for harbor-view rooms in the city. *275 Gloucester Rd. (enter on Cannon St.), 5th Floor. ☎ 852/ 2838-0762. http://home.hkstar.com/ ~alisangh. 21 units. Doubles $HK320. No credit cards. MTR: Causeway Bay. Map p 118.*

★★ **Bishop Lei International House** MID-LEVELS   Some of the rooms at this conveniently located hotel are tiny (welcome to Hong Kong), but they're also comfortable and several have kitchenettes. *4 Robinson Rd. ☎ 852/2868-0828. www.bishopleihtl.com.hk. 219 units. Doubles $HK650–$HK815. AE, DC, MC, V. Bus: 3B, 12, 12M, 23, 23A, or 40 to Robinson Rd. Map p 118.*

★★ kids **Booth Lodge** YAU MA TEI   The Booth Lodge may not offer luxury, but it does offer large rooms that are spotlessly clean and well maintained at very reasonable rates. And it's very conveniently located if you're planning to spend time in Tsim Sha Tsui and Yau Ma Tei. Some of the rooms are a bit noisy, so ask for one facing the hills if you want complete quiet. As an added bonus, local calls are free here, so you don't have to worry about calling ahead to book tickets or check opening and closing hours of shops and museums. *11 Wing Sing Lane. ☎ 852/2771-9266. boothlodge.salvation.org.hk/. 53 units. Doubles HK$420 and up. AE, MC, V. MTR: Yau Ma Tei. Map p 117.*

★ **BP International House** YAU MA TEI   With it's bland beige decor, this homey hotel is far from flashy.

The Bishop Lei International House offers a free shuttle to Central, Admiralty, and Wan Chai.

But the BP offers tidy rooms, most with views of the harbor, and it's got a prime location right near Kowloon Park. *8 Austin Rd. ☎ 852/2376-1111. www.bpih.com.hk. 529 units. Doubles $HK1,400–$HK2,100. AE, DC, MC, V. MTR: Jordan. Map p 117.*

★★ **Conrad Hong Kong** ADMIRALTY   High above shopping haven Pacific Place, this elegant spot is a sea of calm in the center of the city. The rooms are simply done in soothing earth tones, and the lobby has a surprisingly homey feel, with wood paneling and polished granite. *88 Queensway, Pacific Place. ☎ 852/ 2521-3838; ☎ 800/CONRADS in the U.S. and Canada. www.conrad.com. hk. 513 units. Doubles $HK2,850– $HK3,350. AE, DC, MC, V. MTR: Admiralty. Map p 118.*

★★★ **Eaton Hotel** YAU MA TEI
Located above a shopping complex
near the Temple Street Night Market, this hotel is a real find. A four-
story escalator leads to the lobby,
where there's a lounge with free WiFi
service. The rooms are not big, but
the nicest have floor-to-ceiling windows with views of the harbor. The
staff is efficient and always helpful.
380 Nathan Rd. ☎ *852/2782-1818;*
☎ *800/223-5652 in the U.S. and
Canada. www.eaton-hotel.com. 460
units. Single or double $HK1,950–
$2,150. AE, DC, MC, V. MTR: Jordan.
Map p 117.*

★ **Empire Hotel Kowloon** TSIM
SHA TSUI   The rooms located
between the 8th and 26th floors of
this glass tower have floor-to-ceiling
windows, with those above the 17th
floor offering views of the harbor in
the distance. The glass motif continues through the hotel's design,
extending to desktops, tables, and
bathrooms. The pool is, unfortunately, located on the bottom floor,
but with prices far below five-star
hotels, it's a minor detraction from
this modern hotel with reasonable
rates. *62 Kimberley Rd.* ☎ *852/
2685-3000. www.edenhotelgroup.
com. 92 units. Doubles HK$1,600.
AE, DC, MC, V. MTR: TSIM SHA TSUI.
Map p 117.*

A sitting room at the chic Four Seasons.

*You can relax after a day of sightseeing
at the stunning rooftop pool at the Grand
Hyatt. See p 122.*

★★ **The Excelsior** CAUSEWAY BAY
With harbor-view rooms, two excellent bars, and top-notch Chinese and
Italian restaurants, it's no wonder the
Excelsior is always packed. The lobby
and elevators get crowded, but the
rooms have clever design touches,
like couches that are built into the
walls to maximize space. You'll also
have access to a rooftop tennis
court. *281 Gloucester Rd.* ☎ *852/
2894-8888;* ☎ *800/526-6566 in the
U.S. and Canada. www.excelsior
hongkong.com. 863 units. Doubles
$HK1,900–$HK2,700. AE, DC, MC, V.
MTR: Causeway Bay. Map p 118.*

★★★ **Four Seasons Hotel**
CENTRAL   This is a funky hotel
with Chinese artwork on the walls,

marble fittings in the bathrooms, and comfy leather chairs and couches throughout. The hotel is attached to the IFC Mall (you can catch a train to and from the airport here), which can make it feel a bit informal, but the warmth found at the stunning rooftop pool makes up for that. *8 Finance St.* ☎ *852/3196-8888;* ☎ *800/233-1234 in the U.S. and Canda. 399 units. Doubles $HK4,200. AE, DC, MC, V. MTR: Central. Map p 118.*

★★★ **Grand Hyatt** CENTRAL The lobby alone makes this hotel worth a stay: An enormous atrium with black marble floors, glass chandeliers, and curving staircases leading to a restaurant with water views. The rooms are slightly less elegant, but the outdoor pool, with a bubbling fountain, green ferns, and lounge chairs more comfortable than some hotel beds, is a big plus. *1 Harbour Rd.* ☎ *852/2588-1234. www.hongkong.hyatt.com. 572 units. Doubles $HK3,850–$HK4,650. AE, DC, MC, V. MTR: Wan Chai. Map p 118.*

★ **Guangdong Hotel** TSIM SHA TSUI This recently upgraded hotel has an excellent location in the heart of Tsim Sha Tsui. The rooms are small but well kept, though none have views. Still, the prices are low for the area, making it a good bargain. *18 Prat Ave.* ☎ *852/3410-8888.*

The lobby bar at the InterContinental offers amazing city views.

Those who stay at JIA get the VIP treatment, including special access to local clubs.

www.gdhhotels.com. 245 units. Double HK$1,280–$1,780. AE, DC, MC, V. MTR: Tsim Sha Tsui. Map p 117.

★ **Harbor View International House** WAN CHAI The big draw at this YMCA is the fact that more than half the rooms face the water. Granted, the rooms are teeny—all have either twin or double beds—but they're clean and well maintained. The location, in the heart of Wan Chai and right next to the Hong Kong Arts Centre, is convenient, and the prices (especially for rooms with harbor views) simply can't be beat. *4 Harbour Rd.* ☎ *852/2802-0111. www.harbourymca.org.hk. 320 units. HK$1,300–$HK1,950. AE, DC, MC, V. MTR: Wan Chai. Map p 118.*

★ **kids** **Holiday Inn Golden Mile** TSIM SHA TSUI While the decor includes bland colors and ubiquitous hotel art, the rooms are spacious and the staff is helpful. This hotel also offers some surprisingly good dining and entertainment options: The kid-friendly Avenue Restaurant has floor-to-ceiling windows overlooking Nathan and Mody roads, and Hari's at Golden Mile Bar has live music every night. *18 Salisbury Rd.* ☎ *852/2369-3111;* ☎ *800/465-4329 in the U.S. and Canada. www.goldenmile-hk. holiday-inn.com. 600 units. Doubles $HK2,500–$HK2,750. AE, DC, MC, V. MTR: Tsim Sha Tsui. Map p 117.*

★ **Hong Kong Bank Foundation SG Davis Hostel** LANTAU The main reason to stay at this spotless and very inexpensive hostel is its proximity to the top of Lantau Peak. Located far from both the bustle of Hong Kong's urban centers and the small residential areas on Lantau, this place is perfect if you want to hike Lantau Peak in time to watch the sunrise. *Ngong Ping.* ☎ 852/2985-5610. www.yha.org.hk. *46 units. Double room $HK30–$HK45. No credit cards. Bus: Ngong Ping stop. Map p 118.*

★ **Hotel LKF** CENTRAL Lan Kwai Fong (LKF) is party central, but this elegant hotel is surprisingly subdued and the lobby, with its curved walls and dangling silver disks, is space-age cool. Rooms aren't enormous, but space is maximized with flatscreen TVs and built-in shelves. The bathrooms are huge, perfect for primping for an evening out. The final touch is the illy espresso machine in every room. *33 Wyndham St.* ☎ 852/3518-9688. www.hotel-lkf.com.hk. *95 units. Doubles $HK1,950. AE, DC, MC, V. MTR: Central. Map p 118.*

★★★ **InterContinental Hong Kong** TSIM SHA TSUI You'll be impressed the minute you enter this hotel's modern lobby, which has a glass wall revealing Hong Kong's skyline. Rooms are tastefully designed, with silk bedspreads, Asian artwork, and sunken bathtubs, and most have harbor views. It's also home to the world-renowned French-fusion eatery Spoon. *18 Salisbury Rd.* ☎ 852/2721-1211. www.hong kong-ic.intercontinental.com. *514 units. Doubles $HK3,100–$HK3,700. AE, DC, MC, V. MTR: Tsim Sha Tsui. Map p 117.*

★★★ **Island Shangri-La** ADMI-RALTY The Island Shangri-La offers luxury that surprises. A massive painting created by 40 Beijing artists hangs in the 17-story atrium, and Viennese chandeliers illuminate the lobby and many of the rooms. The large rooms feature marble-topped desks, Chinese lacquerware cabinets, and silk bedspreads. *Pacific Place, Supreme Court Rd.* ☎ 852/2877-3838; ☎ 866/565-5050 in the U.S. www. shangri-la.com. *565 units. Doubles $HK2,100–$HK3,450. AE, DC, MC, V. MTR: Admiralty. Map p 118.*

★★ **JIA Boutique Hotel** CAUSE-WAY BAY This Philippe Starck–designed hotel is a modernist dream. The huge rooms have sitting areas separated from sleeping areas by gauzy curtains and marble bathrooms with glass showers and bowl-shaped tubs. The rooms also feature flat-panel TVs, DVD players, and

Rooms at the JW Marriott are designed with right-angle "sawtooth" windows to maximize views. See p 124.

Bedside control panels allow guests at the Langham to operate everything from the TV to the air-conditioning.

surround sound, and local calls are free. *1–5 Irving St.* ☎ *852/3196-9000. www.jiahongkong.com. 57 units. Doubles $HK2,000. AE, DC, MC, V. MTR: Causeway Bay. Map p 118.*

★★ kids **JW Marriott Hong Kong** ADMIRALTY   A great place for families, as the rooms are comfortably spacious, and you can rent video game consoles at the front desk. The outdoor pool is also a treat, as it sits just below Hong Kong Island's green rolling hills. *88 Queensway.* ☎ *852/2810-8366;* ☎ *800/228-9290 5050 in the U.S. and Canada. www.marriotthotels. com. 602 units. Doubles $ HK2,090–$HK3,400. AE, DC, MC, V. MTR: Admiralty. Map p 118.*

★★ **Kowloon Shangri-La** TSIM SHA TSUI   The 21-story Kowloon Shangri-La, like its island-side sister, is a luxury hotel that pays attention

Guests can enjoy the neoclassical charm of the pool at the Mandarin Oriental.

to detail. The elegant lobby is run by an exceedingly friendly staff. The rooms have finely polished wood furniture, marble bathrooms, and views of either the harbor or the surrounding city. There's also a free shuttle to the heart of Tsim Sha Tsui. *64 Mody Rd.* ☎ *852/2721-2111;* ☎ *866/565-5050 in the U.S. www. shangri-la.com. 700 units. Doubles $HK2,650–$HK3,800. AE, DC, MC, V. MTR: Tsim Sha Tsui. Map p 117.*

★★★ **Landmark Mandarin Oriental** CENTRAL   This Peter Remedios–designed hotel, attached to the upscale Landmark Shopping Mall, features sleek curves and gleaming black marble and metal. The rooms are huge by Hong Kong standards, and use design innovations like floating walls to separate sleeping and sitting areas. Added bonus: fine dining options such as Amber (p 83). *15 Queen's Rd.* ☎ *852/2132-0188;* ☎ *800/526-6566 in the U.S. and Canada. www. mandarinoriental.com/landmark. 113 units. Doubles $HK3,000–$HK4,100. AE, DC, MC, V. MTR: Central. Map p 118.*

★★★ **Langham Hotel** TSIM SHA TSUI   This is the only hotel in Hong Kong to belong to The Leading Hotels of the World. From the rooftop pool to the gold-plated fixtures in the marble bathrooms to the hand-painted dome in the lobby, the Langham exudes easy elegance. The rooms are a bit on the small side, but they're well appointed, and the hotel is a quick walk from the Star Ferry. *8 Peking Rd.* ☎ *852/2375-1133;* ☎ *800/223-6800 in the U.S. and Canada. www.langhamhotels.com. 495 units. Single or double $3,400–HK$3,800. AE, DC, MC, V. MTR: Tsim Sha Tsui. Map p 117.*

★★★ Langham Place Hotel

MONGKOK Like the mall it's attached to, this innovative and modern hotel (not to be confused with the Langham Hotel) rises out of the midst of Mongkok, a relatively rundown section of Hong Kong. Standard rooms are stylish, and spa rooms feature Jacuzzi tubs and futon-style beds. But the hotel's best feature may be its view of the streets of Mongkok, where live fish are sold in wet markets and laundry is hung from the windows of decaying apartment blocks. *555 Shanghai St.* ☎ *852/3552-3388. http://hongkong. langhamplacehotels.com. 665 units. Doubles $HK1,400–$HK4,000. AE, DC, MC, V. MTR: Mongkok. Map p 117.*

★★★ Mandarin Oriental CEN-

TRAL This famously posh hotel, opened in 1963 and fully renovated in 2006, has perhaps the most luxurious rooms in Hong Kong—beds piled high with silk pillows, Chinese lacquer furniture, and flatscreen TVs. It's a shame the pool is indoors rather than on the roof, but it's lovely nonetheless. *5 Connaught Rd.* ☎ *852/2522-0111;* ☎ *800/526-6566 in the U.S. and Canada. www. mandarinoriental.com. 502 units. Doubles $HK2,950–$HK4,200. AE, DC, MC, V. MTR: Central. Map p 118.*

★ The Marco Polo Hong Kong

Hotel TSIM SHA TSUI The staff here is so friendly that the marble lobby is often filled with guests asking directions or booking tours. The rooms are subdued but stylish, with large desks, walk-in closets, and sitting areas bigger than most hotel rooms in the city. If you splurge on a luxury harbor view, you're literally on top of the water—ocean liners dock right next to your window. A walkway connects the hotel to the gigantic Harbour City mall. *3 Canton Rd., Harbour City.* ☎ *852/2113-0088;* ☎ *800/448-8355 in the U.S. and Canada. www.marcopolohotels.com. 664 units. Doubles $HK2,400–$HK3,360. AE, DC, MC, V. MTR: Tsim Sha Tsui. Map p 117.*

★★ Metropark Hotel CAUSE-

WAY BAY If you're looking for the conveniences of a modern hotel but want to be a little off the beaten path, the Metropark is for you. The

Even the bathrooms at the Peninsula have great views of the city. See p 126.

design is modern and bright, with plenty of natural sunlight throughout. Though the rooms are small, they're well designed, with separate sitting and sleeping areas. Ask for a room overlooking Victoria Park. *148 Tung Lo Wan Rd.* ☎ *852/2600-1000;* ☎ *800-223-5652 in the U.S. and Canada. www.metroparkhotel.com. 266 units. Doubles $HK1,500–$HK1,800. AE, DC, MC, V. MTR: Tin Hau. Map p 118.*

★ **The Minden** TSIM SHA TSUI The Minden is a quiet surprise amid the crowded streets of Tsim Sha Tsui. The lobby features antique furniture and original artwork. The small rooms are comfortable and chic, with cushy beds, satellite television, and fresh flowers. The hotel also has a funky bar and restaurant. *7 Minden Ave.* ☎ *852/2739-7777. www.theminden.com. 64 units. Doubles $HK900–$HK1,200. AE, MC, V. MTR: Tsim Sha Tsui. Map p 117.*

★ **The Park Lane** CAUSEWAY BAY Some of the decor here is a bit too bold for my tastes, but yellow carpets aside, this hotel fits right in with Causeway Bay's focus on fashion and design. The rooms are stylish, if a bit basic, and they are comfortable and well sized. The views aren't spectacular, but the location is certainly is.

Chinese art decorates the walls of the Renaissance Harbour View's lobby.

310 Gloucester Rd. ☎ *852/2293-8888;* ☎ *800/457-4000 in the U.S. and Canada. www.parklane.com.hk. 803 units. Doubles $HK2,000–$HK3,100. AE, DC, MC, V. MTR: Causeway Bay. Map p 118.*

★★★ **The Peninsula** TSIM SHA TSUI The Peninsula lives up to its reputation as one of the best hotels in Hong Kong. Built in the 1920s, it has maintained a classic feel while completely modernizing. The lobby is ornate, as are the rooms, which have dark-wood furnishings, Chinese art, and remote controls for the TV and radio inlaid into panels by the bed. There's also a stunning indoor pool. It's pricey, but you won't wonder why. *Salisbury Rd.* ☎ *852/2920-2888;* ☎ *800/462-7899 in the U.S. and Canada. www.peninsula.com. 300 units. Doubles $HK3,000–$HK4,900. AE, DC, MC, V. MTR: Tsim Sha Tsui. Map p 117.*

Regal Airport Hotel LANTAU Just a 5-minute walk from the terminals, this is the place to stay if you have an early morning flight. The rooms are dull but spacious and soundproof; many have views of the landing strip. The hotel also features five restaurants, indoor and outdoor pools, a health club and spa, a children's recreation room, and a shopping arcade. *Hong Kong International Airport.* ☎ *852/2286-8888. www.regalhotel.com. 1,104 units. Doubles $HK1,700–$HK2,950. AE, DC, MC, V. Map p 118.*

★★★ **kids Renaissance Harbour View Hotel** WAN CHAI This hotel has a spacious lobby with a lounge and bar overlooking the harbor. The rooms are havens of quiet, with plenty of space to spread out, making it an especially great spot for families. And even if you don't score a harbor view, you'll overlook lush gardens. There's also an outdoor pool that looks out at the

The Ritz-Carlton has a calm, quiet atmosphere that's a far cry from much of Hong Kong's hustle and bustle.

surrounding skyscrapers. With prices nearly half of the adjacent Grand Hyatt's, it's a terrific value. *1 Harbour Rd.* ☎ *852/2802-8888;* ☎ *800/228-9290 in the U.S. and Canada. www.renaissancehotels.com. 862 units. $HK2,300–$HK2,700. AE, DC, MC, V. MTR: Wan Chai. Map p 118.*

★★★ kids The Ritz-Carlton

CENTRAL   The simple yet elegant rooms at this luxury hotel face either the harbor or the Peak, and either way, the views are excellent. So is the service—if you're traveling with small children, for example, the hotel will install safety devices like electric outlet plugs when you check in. The lobby features an extensive collection of 18th- and 19th-century artwork and antiques and the spa even offers a chocolate facial. *3 Connaught Rd.* ☎ *852/2877-6666;* ☎ *800/241-3333 in the U.S. and Canada. www.ritz carlton.com. 216 units. Singles and doubles $HK3,600–$HK4,100, AE, DC, MC, V. MTR: Central. Map p 118.*

★ Rosedale on the Park

CAUSEWAY BAY   The Rosedale is a wonderful place to stay in the center of Causeway Bay. There's free WiFi in the rooms, free drinks in the fridge when you check in, and even in-house mobile phones that allow you to get calls when you're not in

your room (but still in the hotel). Some rooms have kitchenettes and dining tables, making them feel more like apartments. *8 Shelter St.* ☎ *852/2127-8888;* ☎ *800/521-5200 in the U.S. and Canada. www.rosedale.com.hk. 274 units. Doubles $HK1,280–$HK1,380. AE, DC, MC, V. MTR: Causeway Bay. Map p 118.*

★★ Royal Garden TSIM SHA TSUI

This small hotel has one of the cooler interiors in Hong Kong. Rooms open onto a 15-story inner atrium modeled after traditional Chinese inner gardens. The rooms are great too, though you won't get much of a view of the nearby harbor. You will get a mix of modern and colonial furniture, a plasma TV, and a chilled, purified water tap in the bathroom. *69 Mody Rd.* ☎ *852/2721-5215;* ☎ *800/448-8355 in the U.S. www.rghk.com.hk. 422 units. Doubles $HK2,450–$HK3,150. AE, DC, MC, V. MTR: Tsim Sha Tsui. Map p 117.*

★ kids The Salisbury YMCA

TSIM SHA TSUI   Don't want to spring for the Peninsula, but envy its location? The Salisbury's simple but spotless rooms are the answer. With a pool, a restaurant, and even a climbing wall, it's a good value—and great if you have kids, as you can get larger rooms for less than

The inner atrium is one of the big draws at the Royal Garden. See p 127.

you would elsewhere. *41 Salisbury Rd. 852/2268-7000. www.ymcahk. org.hk. 363 units. Doubles $HK800–$HK1,000. AE, DC, MC, V. MTR: Tsim Sha Tsui. Map p 117.*

★★★ Sheraton Hong Kong Hotel
TSIM SHA TSUI   The modern rooms here feature marble bathrooms and plush bedding, and extras include a year-round, rooftop swimming pool. The Sheraton doesn't have the history of the Peninsula or the fun surprises of the Intercontinental, but it's a bit cheaper and still offers luxury and convenience. *20 Nathan Rd. 852/2369-1111; 800/462-7899 in the U.S. and Canada. www.sheraton.com/ hongkong. 780 units. Doubles $HK2,700–$HK3,400. AE, DC, MC, V. MTR: Tsim Sha Tsui. Map p 117.*

★ Stanford Hillview Hotel
TSIM SHA TSUI   This intimate little hotel manages to provide the best of both worlds in terms of location. It's in the heart of bustling Tsim Sha Tsui, but it stands a bit apart, under some banyan trees in a quiet spot on a hill next to the Royal Observatory. The rooms are small and basic—most have twin beds—but the staff is friendly and the vibe here is far more laid-back than you're likely to find anywhere else in the neighborhood. There's a small kitchen for guests to use. *13-17 Observatory Rd. 852/2722-7822. www.stanfordhillview.com. 163 units. HK$1,000-HK$1,680. AE, DC, MC, V. MTR: Tsim Sha Tsui. Map p 117.* ●

Macau

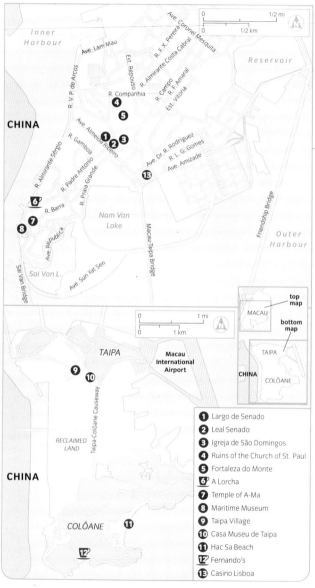

1. Largo de Senado
2. Leal Senado
3. Igreja de São Domingos
4. Ruins of the Church of St. Paul
5. Fortaleza do Monte
6. A Lorcha
7. Temple of A-Ma
8. Maritime Museum
9. Taipa Village
10. Casa Museu de Taipa
11. Hac Sa Beach
12. Fernando's
13. Casino Lisboa

Previous page: Buddha, as carved into a rock wall in Shenzhen.

Macau is best known for its hugely successful gambling scene—word has it that more money changes hands here than in Las Vegas—but there's a lot more to this island. Macau was controlled by Portugal until 1999, when it was handed back to China, and there's a real mix of cultures here. Thanks to its status as a duty-free port, it's a shopping mecca (you can use Hong Kong dollars pretty much everywhere). You'll also find colonial architecture, excellent food, and of course, the ubiquitous casinos. Macau is only 45 minutes away by high-speed ferry, which means you can spend a full day and evening here and be back in Hong Kong in time for bed. If you'd rather spend the night, some hotel suggestions are listed at the end of this section. START: **Macau Ferry Pier.**

❶ ★★★ **Largo de Senado (Senate Square).** In Macau's central square, brightly painted colonial buildings from the late 1700s now house Western staples like Starbucks and the Body Shop. But even the modern-day commerce doesn't detract from the lovely architecture. There's an information booth for visitors in the center of the square. ⏱ *20 min. Avenida de Almedia Ribeiro. Bus: 3, 3A, 4, 5, 7, 8, 10, 10A, 10B, 11, 21, 21A, 26, 26A, or 33.*

The vibrantly colored buildings in Macau's Largo de Senado are a remnant of the Portuguese influence here.

Pedicabs, like this one parked outside the Leal Senado, were a common form of transportation in Macau until the 1980s.

❷ ★ **Leal Senado (Loyal Senate).** Built in the 1780s and facing the Largo de Senado, this was the seat of the Portuguese colonial government; today, it houses the offices of the mayor. Inside is an art gallery with historical paintings of Macau, as well as an ornately furnished Senate Library. The garden at the back is small but beautifully landscaped, with a bronze bust of Luis de Camoes, the 14th-century Portuguese poet. ⏱ *30 min. 163 Avenida de Almedia Ribeiro. Gallery Tues–Sun 9am–9pm; library Mon–Sat 1–7pm. Free admission. Bus: 3, 3A, 4, 5,7, 8, 10, 10A, 10B, 11, 21, 21A, 26, 26A, or 33.*

A detail from the facade of the Igreja de São Domingos (Church of St. Dominic).

③ ★ Igreja de São Domingos (Church of St. Dominic). This yellow church with square, green doors dates back to the 17th century. Inside, rows of pews stretch along the green interior to a majestic altar where a crucifix hangs. The upper floors house the Tesouraria de Arte Sacra (Treasury of Sacred Art which has religious paraphernalia from the start of missionary work in Macau, including clerical vestments, bronze church bells, and statues of saints. Downstairs an exhibit details the construction of the church. ⏱ *30*

min. Largo de São Domingos. ☎ *853/ 2836-7706. Church daily 8am–6pm; Tesouraria de Arte Sacra daily 10am–6pm. Bus: 3, 3A, 4, 5, 7, 8, 10, 10A, 10B, 11, 21, 21A, 26, 26A, or 33.*

④ ★★★ Ruins of the Church of St. Paul. Although only the facade of this late-14th-century church remains, it is still the grandest sight in Macau, sitting atop a large stone staircase and overlooking the city below. Designed by an Italian Jesuit and constructed by exiled Japanese Christians, it was the largest Catholic Church in Asia until it was decimated by a typhoon in the 1830s. Today, you can walk around the stone foundations admiring the baroque facade with its elaborate carvings of saints. ⏱ *20 min. Rua de São Paulo.* ☎ *853/2835-8444. Museum daily 9am–6pm. Bus: 8A, 17, 18, 19, or 26.*

⑤ ★★ Fortaleza do Monte (Monte Forte). The walls of this fort formed the boundaries of the original Portuguese settlement in Macau in the early 1600s. In modern times, the colonial government's military was based here until 1966, when the government became more diplomatic in their dealings with China. Today, the fort offers wonderful views of Macau from behind old canons and parapets. It also houses the Macau Museum, which gives a

Getting There

Even though Macau is part of China, you must have your passport with you to buy a ticket to go there. Two ferry terminals service Macau in Hong Kong: one in Sheung Wan and the other in Tsim Sha Tsui. The one in Sheung Wan (200 Connaught Rd.) is the most convenient, with ferries leaving for the island every half-hour, 24 hours a day. I suggest taking the **TurboJET,** which takes only an hour to reach the island (☎ 852/2859-3333; www.turbojet.com.hk; one-way fares Mon–Fri \$HK243 for super class, \$HK141 for economy class; Sat–Sun \$HK259 and \$HK153).

The front wall is all that remains standing of the Church of St. Paul.

detailed history of the territory in slides and photographs. ⏱ *45 min. 112 Praceta do Museu de Macau.* ☎ *853/2835-7911. www.macau museum.gov.mo. Tues–Sun 10am–6pm. Admission $HK15 adults; $HK8 kids. Bus: 8A, 17, 18, 19, or 26.*

⑥ ★★ **A Lorcha.** The Portuguese food at this small, whitewashed restaurant is superb, with dishes such as codfish in a cream sauce, baked minced beef potato pie, and char-grilled king prawns. Its name refers to a Portuguese junk or sailboat, which is fitting considering its proximity to the ocean. *289A Rua do Almirante Sergio.* ☎ *853/2831-3193. $$.*

⑦ ★★ **Temple of A-Ma.** This is Macau's oldest Chinese temple, with some parts dating back more than 600 years. It is dedicated to A-Ma, the Chinese goddess of seafarers, and has a large boulder in front with a colored relief of a lorcha, or traditional sailing junk. Midway up the stone steps you'll find an altar for burning incense and praying to A-Ma—farther up are more altars,

where the faithful ask for good luck from their ancestors. There are often fireworks displays here; traditionally they were used to scare off evil spirits. ⏱ *45 min. Rua de S. Tiago da Barra. Daily 6:30am–6pm. Bus: 1, 1A, 2, 5, 6, 7, 9, 10, 10A, 11, 18, 21, 21A, 28B, or 34.*

⑧ ★★ **Maritime Museum.** This museum showcases Macau's long relationship with the sea. You'll find an exhibit using replicas of boats to show how fishermen worked and lived and a maritime history section that illustrates the routes explorers took to reach Macau. There's also a small aquarium with fish native to the area. ⏱ *45 min. Rua de Sao Tiago da Barra.* ☎ *853/2859-9548. Tues–Sat 10:30am–5:30pm. Admission $HK10 adults; $HK5 kids 10–17; free for children under 10.*

⑨ ★★ **Taipa Village.** This small, traditional community—on an island connected to the peninsula by bridges—is made up of narrow lanes and colonial buildings painted Portuguese style in yellows, blues, and greens. Most people now live in the surrounding housing projects, but

Fireworks hang at the Temple of A-Ma.

you'll still see residents carrying vegetables and goods in wicker baskets balanced on poles across their shoulders, just as they did hundreds of years ago. 45 min. Rua do Sol. Bus: 11, 15, 22, 28A, 30, 33, 34, or 35.

🔟 ★★ Casa Museu da Taipa (Taipa House Museum). Built in the early 1920s, this colonial-style building was the summer home of a wealthy Macanese family. Now a museum, it has period paintings, furniture, and personal artifacts on display. 1 hr. Avenida da Praia. ☎ 853/2882-7088. Tues–Sun 10am–6pm. Admission $HK5. Bus: 11, 15, 22, 28A, 30, 33, or 34.

⓫ ★ Hac Sa Beach. A small, serene black sand beach with views of the South China Sea, Hac Sa is a great place for a break. 2 hr. Coloane Village. Bus: 21A or 26A.

⓬ ★★★ Fernando's. It doesn't look like much from the outside, but once you taste the Portuguese food served here, you won't care. The best dish is the charcoal-grilled

Diners dig in at Fernando's, which sits right on the beach at Hac Sa.

chicken, closely followed by the Portuguese chorizo, codfish, and mussels. The bread comes from the restaurant's bakery and the vegetables are from its garden across the border in China. *Praia de Hac Sa.* ☎ 852/2888-2264. $$

An altar at a temple in Taipa, an island that is home to 42,000 residents.

⑬ ★ Casino Lisboa. Casino Lisboa has been a Macau staple since the 1970s, and it's about as un–Las Vegas as it gets. Drinking is at a minimum and "no smoking" rules don't apply—people puff away as they gamble here. There are glitzier places to visit, but this is the most uniquely Chinese. The casino is even rumored to have been built with feng shui that favors the house. ◔ 1 hr. 2–4 Avenida de Lisboa. ☎ 853/2888-3888. www.hotelisboa.com.

If you're looking for an authentically Chinese gambling experience, head to Casino Lisboa.

Where to Stay

★★ Hotel Guia MACAU PENINSULA If you're looking for a quiet retreat at a reasonable price, this lovely hotel it. Surrounded by traditional colonial architecture, the Hotel Guia sits on the slope of Guia Hill, below the Guia Fort and Lighthouse. The staff is warm and helpful and the rooms are spotless (ask for a room with a view of the lighthouse and harbor). You're a bit far from the roar of Macau's nightlife, but that's not necessarily a bad thing. *Estrada do Engenheiro Trigo, 1–5.* ☎ *853/2851-3888. www.hotelguia-macau.com. 90 units. Doubles HK$880–HK$1,080. Bus: 28C.*

★★★ Mandarin Oriental Macau MACAU PENINSULA Although this Mandarin Oriental has the same great service and style as the ones in Hong Kong, it's a bit cheaper and has the added bonus of being located just 7 minutes from Macau's ferry terminal. The spacious rooms are decorated with Portuguese fabrics and teakwood furnishings. *956–1110 Av. da Amizade.* ☎ *853/2856-7888. www.mandarinoriental.com/macau. 435*

units. Doubles HK$2,000–HK$2,600. Bus: 10A or 10B.

★★★ Pousada de Mong Ha MACAU PENINSULA This is a wonderful hotel for the price. Run by the Instituto de Formacao Turistica (Institute for Tourism Studies), the hotel has a pleasant and quiet setting, the staff is attentive, and the rooms are cozy. *Colina de Mong Ha.* ☎ *853/2851-5222. www.ift.edu.mo/pousada/eng/enchantment.htm. 20 units. Doubles HK$600–HK$800. Bus: 12.*

★★ Pousada de São Tiago MACAU PENINSULA Built around the ruins of the Portuguese Fortress da Barra, which dates to 1629, this dramatic beach hotel has a secluded, romantic feel. Little wonder, then, that it's such a popular wedding destination. The rooms are filled with ornately carved Portuguese furniture, and almost all have balconies overlooking the sea. *Av. Da Republica, Fortaleza de Sao Tiago da Barra.* ☎ *853/2837-8111. www.saotiago.com.mo. 24 units. Doubles HK$2,600-HK$3,200. Bus: 28B.*

Shenzhen

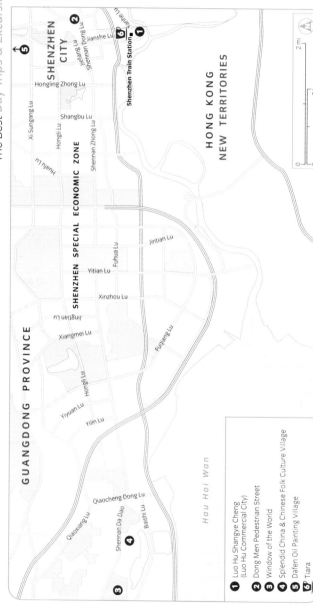

SHENZHEN CITY

SHENZHEN SPECIAL ECONOMIC ZONE

GUANGDONG PROVINCE

HONG KONG NEW TERRITORIES

Hau Hoi Wan

Shenzhen Train Station

Hongling Zhong Lu
Shangbu Lu
Shennan Zhong Lu
Hongli Lu
Huaiqiang Lu
Jianshe Lu
Jiefang Lu
Shennan Dong Lu
Jiabin Lu

Huala Lu
Xiangmei Lu
Hongli Lu
Yiyuan Lu
Yilin Lu
Jingtian Lu
Xinzhou Lu
Yitian Lu
Fuhua Lu
Jintian Lu
Fuqiang Lu

Qiaocheng Dong Lu
Qiaoxiang Lu
Shennan Da Dao
Baishi Lu

1. Luo Hu Shangye Cheng
   (Luo Hu Commercial City)
2. Dong Men Pedestrian Street
3. Window of the World
4. Splendid China & Chinese Folk Culture Village
5. Dafen Oil Painting Village
6. Tiara

0   2 km
0   2 mi

As one of China's initial Special Economic Zones, Shenzhen was among the first places in China to open itself to the West, both economically and culturally, in the late 1970s. Today, this skyscraper-filled city has become a major destination for tourists who want to get a taste of mainland China—and do some serious discount shopping—during a visit to Hong Kong. The prices are low, and despite a police crackdown on counterfeit goods, they're still relatively easy to find. Just keep in mind, you'll need a visa from the Chinese consulate in order to go and you must change your Hong Kong dollars for Chinese yuan (see "Getting There," p 139). START: **Lo We Border Crossing.**

❶ ★ Luo Hu Shangye Cheng (Luo Hu Commercial City). A multilevel shopping center, loaded with stalls and shops selling everything from purses to massages to pirated DVDs, Luo Hu offers some great deals. The dealers here can be aggressive, but stay firm. Unlike Hong Kong, all the prices here are negotiable, even in the shops. ⏱ *1 hr. Metro station: Luoho, exit A. Daily 8:30am–11:30pm.*

❷ ★★ Dong Men Pedestrian Street. Once blocked from car traffic, this shopping area was a working town more than 300 years ago. Shopping here is more like a sport, with haggling merchants and tailors competing for your attention (and dollars). Always try on clothing before buying, as Chinese cuts often mean small sleeves for men and tiny waists for women. ⏱ *2 hr. Dongmen District, Laojie metro station, north of Shennan Dong Rd.*

❸ Window of the World. This park is worth visiting not so much for its intended purpose—to wow you with its replicas of the world's great sites—but as a revealing look at the tourism industry in China, which veers toward the campy and outlandish. Here, you'll find a miniature Eiffel Tower, an Egyptian pyramid, and the Taj Mahal. Live shows throughout the day celebrate various world cultures—though not always accurately. Other wacky offerings include indoor skiing on a tiny hill and learning to hunt like a Native American. ⏱ *1 hr. Overseas Chinese Town.* ☎ *755/2660-8000. Mon–Fri*

Not an inch of advertising space is wasted at Luo Hu Shangye Cheng, one of Shenghesn's largest shopping centers.

A miniature Taj Mahal is just one of the oddities found at Window of the World.

9am–9pm; Sat–Sun 9am–10:30pm. Subway: Line 1 to Shi Ji Zhi Chuang. Bus: 20, 21, 26, 204, 209, 210, 222, 223, 101, 105, 113, 301, 310, 311, 320, 324, 328, 329 or 370.

❹ Splendid China & Chinese Folk Culture Village. This park is, first and foremost, meant to show that China embraces its large population of ethnic minorities despite accusations of human rights abuses from the international community. Unfortunately, many of the exhibits misrepresent these minorities, showing them as leading perfect, tranquil lives free of poverty and hardship. Still, you'll get some idea of China's varied population, with exhibits showing the wardrobes, rituals, and songs of 56 different ethnic groups ranging from the Dai in Yunna Province to the Mongols in

Models of China's famous terra-cotta warriors are on display at Splendid China & Chinese Folk Culture Village.

the north. 🕒 *1 hr. Overseas Chinese Town.* ☎ *755/2692-6808. Mon–Fri 10am–10:30pm; Sat–Sun 10am–8pm. Admission $HK116. Subway: Line 1 to Shi Ji Zhi Chuang. Bus: 20, 21, 26, 204, 209, 210, 222, 223, 101, 105, 113, 301, 310, 311, 320, 324, 328, 329, or 370.*

❺ Dafen Oil Painting Village. If you think copying movies is unethical, you'll want to skip Dafen, where hundreds of artists duplicate classic Western paintings ranging from works by van Gogh to Miró. Luckily, they also do some original work which is worth checking out. 🕒 *2 hr. B-930, ZhenYe Mansion, Bao'An Rd.* ☎ *755/2586-3235. www.chinae.com. cn/com/dafen/main.php. Take taxi from border or center of Shenzhen.*

❻ ★★ Tiara. Located on the 31st floor of the Shangri-La Hotel, this luxurious restaurant slowly rotates to reveal Shenzhen's eclectic skyline—from shiny glass buildings to massive billboards to flashing neon signs. The restaurant serves a wide variety of food, including an international buffet with seafood, fish, and chicken. There's also hotpot, a Chinese meal where you get plates of thinly sliced raw meat and vegetables for you to cook yourself in a spicy broth. *East Side, Railway Station 1002 Jianshe Rd.* ☎ *755/8233-0888. $$$.*

Getting There

You need a visa to visit Shenzhen, but they're not hard to get. Go to the China visa office (26 Harbour Rd., 7th Floor, Wan Chai; ☎ 852/3413-2424), and allow 3 days for processing. You can also join a tour, which will take care of visa issues for you. The **China Travel Service** (C.T.S. House, 78–83 Connaught Rd., Central; ☎ 852/2853-3888; www.ctshk.com/english/index.htm) offers a number of options to Shenzhen and other parts of China. **Oriental Travel** (80 Queen's Rd. East, Room 1901, Wan Chai; ☎ 852/2865-2618; www.orientaltravel.com) also offers Shenzhen tours and often has good deals. The easiest way to get to Shenzhen on your own is to hop the Kowloon-Canton Railway to the border crossing at Lo Wu (one-way is $HK73 for adults, HK37 for children).

Once in Shenzhen, you'll need to use mainland Chinese yuan—there are money exchanges at the border as well as ATMs. The exchange rate is $HK1 to .97 yuan, or US$1 to 7.6 yuan.

An artist is hard at work on a copy of a Miró painting at the Dafen Oil Painting Village.

Cheung Chau

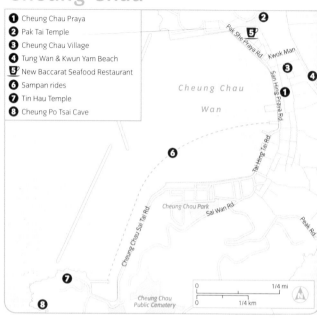

1 Cheung Chau Praya
2 Pak Tai Temple
3 Cheung Chau Village
4 Tung Wan & Kwun Yam Beach
5 New Baccarat Seafood Restaurant
6 Sampan rides
7 Tin Hau Temple
8 Cheung Po Tsai Cave

Once a refuge for pirates (like the legendary 19th-century buccaneer Cheung Po Tsai, who used it as a hideout), Cheung Chau is a fascinating little island where fishing families still live on junks in the harbor. The main village is a warren of narrow lanes where you can get everything from dried seafood to a haircut, and you'll get a real feel for rural Cantonese life. There are no cars, but the island is easy to walk or bike around. START: **Cheung Chau Ferry Pier.**

1 **Cheung Chau Praya.** Exiting the ferry, you'll spot some things (like ATMs and a McDonald's) that normally send up tourist-trap warning flags. Don't be alarmed. The Praya, a harbor-side promenade, is the only place on Cheung Chau with this kind of Western atmosphere. It's also the best spot to rent bikes, if you'd rather ride than walk. ⏱ *1 hr.* ☎ *852/2131-8181. www.cheungchau.org. Outlying Islands Ferry: 5 from Central; fast and slow ferries run all day.*

2 **Pak Tai Temple.** Built in 1783, this large temple is the focus of the Bun Festival in late April or May, which features a 15m-high (50-ft.) tower of steamed buns. The temple is dedicated to Pak Tai, Taoist god of the sea and "Supreme Emperor of the Dark Heaven." He's not as ominous as he sounds—he's basically the guardian of peace. Inside is a 1,000-year-old iron sword nearly 2m (5-ft.) long found by local fishermen. ⏱ *30 min.*

③ Cheung Chau Village. The narrow, winding streets of this village are filled with shops selling medicinal herbs, fish, and other local goods. Watch for homes with small altars open to the street—families leave offerings to their ancestors in exchange (they hope) for good luck. ⏱ *1 hr.*

④ Tung Wan & Kwun Yam Beach. This small beach is a prime windsurfing spot. If you want to give it a try, the Cheung Chau Windsurfing Center rents boards and offers lessons. Otherwise just relax on the sand and enjoy the free show. ⏱ *2 hr. Cheung Chau Windsurfing Center* ☎ *852/2981-8316. Rentals start at $HK110 for 2 hr.*

⑤ New Baccarat Seafood Restaurant. This open-air restaurant sits at the end of the Praya, and has a view of the harbor. It's run by a fishing family, and it has tanks of live sea creatures on display, so you know the fish is fresh. Try the steamed fish or the prawns made with garlic and spices. *9A Pak She Praya St.* ☎ *852/2981-0606. $$.*

Sticks of incense burn in a stone urn outside the Pak Tai Temple.

Paper lanterns for sale in Cheung Chau Village.

⑥ Sampan Rides. It's easy to flag down a *kai do,* or water taxi, along the Praya and it's the best way to see the southwestern peninsula of the island, called Sai Wan. The trip usually lasts 10 minutes or so and costs only $HK5. ⏱ *30 min. Cheung Chau Praya.*

⑦ Tin Hau Temple. This temple, located just off the ferry pier, isn't much different from the many temples around Hong Kong dedicated to Tin Hau, goddess of the sea and protector of fishermen and women, but it's a lovely place to absorb the island's quiet calm. ⏱ *15 min.*

⑧ Cheung Po Tsai Cave. Legend has it that pirate Cheung Po Tsai once commanded 600 junks and had a gang of 4,000 men. He terrorized the seas until 1810, when he surrendered to the Chinese government and became (what else?) an official. But he first hid his treasure, perhaps near this cave, which he used as a hiding place. If you're interested in spelunking, consider that the cave requires patience and a lack of claustrophobia as you inch your way through its very tight spaces. Be careful as the rocks can be slippery. ⏱ *45 min.*

Peng Chau

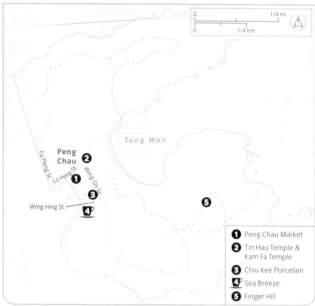

1. Peng Chau Market
2. Tin Hau Temple & Kam Fa Temple
3. Chiu Kee Porcelain
4. Sea Breeze
5. Finger Hill

Peng Chau is a tiny, gorgeously green island that doesn't draw big crowds from Hong Kong. With a population of just 7,800, the island has retained much of its Chinese heritage, and the streets are filled with the smell of fresh fish and the clatter of mahjong tiles. It's easy to lose yourself as you wander the island. Just be sure to keep an eye on the time—the ferries stop running at night. START: **Peng Chau Pier.**

Getting There

Since Peng Chau is far less visited than some of Hong Kong's other outlying islands, you may have trouble getting there. But have no fear—it's easy. Just head to the Central ferry terminal and catch Ferry 5. Boats run back and forth all day (though not at night).

1. ★ **Peng Chau Market.** You've likely already visited a wet market during your time in Hong Kong, but this one feels more vibrant than those in the city. It features live fish, fresh fruit and vegetables, and plenty of cooking spices and herbs. *1 hr. See "Getting There," for information on getting to Peng Chau.*

2. ★★ **Tin Hau Temple & Kam Fa Temple.** The Tin Hau Temple was built in 1792 and is, like most such places in Hong Kong, an active place for prayer. But this pretty little temple has something the others

A traditional Chinese junk is moored in Peng Chau's harbor.

don't: a 2m (8 ft.) whale bone, blackened by incense smoke, which serves as an offering to the gods in return for keeping the island's inhabitants safe and prosperous. Nearby is the smaller, less colorful Kam Fa Temple. Kam Fa is a goddess who is said to have learned kung fu in order to steal from the rich and give to the poor. ⏱ *45 min.*

③ Chiu Kee Porcelain. Chiu Kee Porcelain is said to be the only hand-painted porcelain factory left in Hong Kong (the porcelain industry once dominated this region, but it is now based on the mainland). The owner, Lam Hon-chiu, came here from mainland China during the Communist purges of 1957, and though he no longer paints the teapots, cups, and plates for sale here himself, his wife continues the tradition. ⏱ *45 min. Shop 7, Wing Hing St.* ☎ *852/2983-0917.*

④ Sea Breeze. There aren't all that many restaurant options on Peng Chau, so your choices are a bit limited. Sea Breeze is a small eatery serving well-prepared international fare, including steaks and pasta dishes. It also has outdoor seating with a view of the water. *38 Wing Hing St.* ☎ *852/2983-1787. $$.*

⑤ ★★★ Finger Hill. At 95m (312 ft.), this is the highest point on the island. An incredibly verdant trail takes you to the top, where a small pavilion offers a place to sit and admire the views. You'll see the ocean, the island, and Hong Kong Island from a southeastern perspective—something most Hong Kong visitors never get to see. ⏱ *2 hr.*

A Chinese fisherwoman carries her bundles the old-fashioned way as she walks up a wooden gangplank.

Lamma

1 Yung Shue Wan
2 Bookworm Cafe
3 Hung Shing Yeh Beach
4 Family Trail
5 Sok Kwu Wan Tin Hau Temple
6 Lo So Shing Beach
7 Sok Kwu Wan
8 Lamma Fisherfolk's Village
9 Rainbow Seafood Restaurant

Lamma, one of Hong Kong's 260 outlying islands, is just a short boat ride from the city, but it feels like it's light years from the hubbub of urban life. Lamma is largely undeveloped (there are no cars on the island), but there are two main villages, connected by a lovely 90-minute hike. Slow- and high-speed ferries stop at both villages, so I suggest heading to Yung Shue Wan and then walking to Sok Kwu Wan for dinner before catching a ride back to Hong Kong.

START: **Yung Shue Wan Pier.**

❶ **Yung Shue Wan.** The most inhabited part of Lamma, Yung Shue Wan, or "Banyan Tree Bay," has a cluster of shops, restaurants, bars, and a few small hotels, all catering to tourists. There's a laid-back vibe here—proof that Hong Kong is not all banks and skyscrapers. Stroll the winding streets and enjoy the shops before heading to tiny Tin Hau Temple, on the water's edge. Tin Hau is the goddess of the sea. This temple was built more than 150 years ago, and it is still used for prayer by locals. ⏲ *2 hr. www.lamma.com.hk. Outlying Islands Ferry: 4 from Central; fast and slow ferries run all day.*

The ❷ **Bookworm Cafe** is a real find. Located beyond the more touristy seafood places, this vegetarian restaurant is the informal meeting place for the island's large

Fishing boats dominate the sleepy harbor at Yung Shu Wan on Lamma.

expat community. It's easy to see why: A range of books and magazines line the walls of the small dining room, the menu is eclectic (everything from pancakes to vegetarian lasagna), and there's even an outdoor terrace. *79 Main St. ☎ 852/2982-4838. $$.*

❸ **Hung Shing Yeh Beach.** This is Lamma's most popular beach, thanks mostly to its proximity to town. Though the island's power station smokestacks do intrude on the otherwise stunning view of the ocean and surrounding hills, the beach has a lot to offer. It's broad enough to accommodate the crowds that gather here on hot days, and it's kept spotlessly clean. A nearby beach resort offers drinks and there are free showers and changing rooms. ⏲ *1 hr.*

❹ **Family Trail.** At the far end of Hung Shing Yeh Beach, you'll see a modern pagoda overlooking the South China Sea. That's the entrance to the slightly hilly, paved trail that will take you to the other side of the island. The walk takes about 90 minutes, and along the way, you'll climb to the top of a barren hill before descending through lush banana groves. You'll get some excellent views of the island and some gorgeous glimpses of the ocean. The hike is never truly strenuous, but it can be trying on a hot day, so bring water. ⏲ *90 min.*

Worshippers light thick sticks of incense at the Sok Kwu Wan Temple.

⑤ Sok Kwu Wan Tin Hau Temple.

Near the end of Family Trail, you'll come to the 150-year-old Sok Kwu Wan Tin Hau Temple—yet another temple dedicated to the goddess of the sea. Locals often gather out front to play mahjong or Chinese chess. The original building was destroyed by a fire in 2004, but it has since been reconstructed. The new building contains a bell and altar from the original. *20 min.*

⑥ Lo So Shing Beach.

This beach is truly a gem. It's one of the least populated beaches around—enjoy the solitude while you can. The beach is small, but there are life-guards and changing rooms. If you want a break from the sun, head for the back of the beach, where the surrounding trees provide plenty of cooling shade. *2 hr.*

⑦ Sok Kwu Wan.

This long stretch of pier is crammed with open-air restaurants serving fresh fish, abalone, and shrimp and lob-sters caught in local waters. The seafood is typically prepared Can-tonese style—meaning lots of garlic, spices, and accompanying bowls of steamed rice. Ignore the touts who try to entice you into their places, and take your time checking out the tanks of live seafood that each place has out on display. *30 min.*

⑧ Lamma Fisherfolk's Village.

Sok Kwu Wan's harbor is home to Hong Kong's largest fleet of fish-breeding rafts, some of which also support family homes. This floating "village," reached by shuttle from the public pier, consists of moorings, fish-breeding rafts, and displays relating to local fisherfolk culture. There's even a 60-year-old junk you can explore. *90 min. Sok Kwu Wan Harbor.* ☎ 852/2982-8585. www.fisherfolks.com.hk. Admission, including shuttle, $HK40.

⑨ Rainbow Seafood Restaurant

is the largest open-air restaurant on Sok Kwu Kan's waterfront—just look for the whirling ceiling fans and the red lanterns out in front. It also hap-pens to have one of the best views of the harbor and an English-language menu with plenty of pictures of its main dishes. The food is excellent—the specialties include grilled lobster and fried crab with ginger and scal-lions. Best of all, the restaurant offers free ferry service back to Queen's Pier in Central and Tsim Sha Tsui's public pier—just be sure you make a reservation. *17 1st St, Sok Kwu Wan waterfront.* ☎ 852/2982-8100. www.rainbowrest.com.hk. $$. ●

Seafood doesn't get any fresher than at the markets and restaurants along the piers at Sok Kwu Wan.

Before You Go

Government Tourist Offices
IN THE U.S.: 115 East 54th St., 2nd
Floor, New York, NY 10022-4512
(☎ 212/421-3382); 10940 Wilshire
Blvd., Suite 2050, Los Angeles, CA
90024-3915 (☎ 310/208-4582); 130
Montgomery St., San Francisco, CA
94104 (☎ 415/781-4587). **IN
CANADA:** 9 Temperance St.,
Ground Floor, Toronto, Ontario M5H
1Y6 (☎ 416/366-2389). **IN THE
U.K.:** 6 Grafton St., London W1S
4EQ (☎ 020/7533-7100). **IN AUS-
TRALIA:** Level 4, Hong Kong House,
80 Druitt St., Sydney, NSW 2000
(☎ 02/9283-3083).

The Best Times to Go
It's best to visit Hong Kong in the
autumn or spring, when tempera-
tures are mild. The summers are
hot, humid, and generally quite
uncomfortable, but everyplace from
public buses to small shops are air-
conditioned, which helps. It's wise
to book ahead no matter when you
go, because conferences and mainland Chinese tourists keep the city
busy year-round. If you can, avoid
"Golden Weeks," when all of mainland China is on vacation. These
start May 1 and October 1.

Festivals & Special Events
SPRING. The **Hong Kong Rugby
World Cup Sevens** (☎ 852/2504-
8311; www.hksevens.com.hk) is a
major expat event—and a major
excuse for beer drinking. Rugby
teams from around the world come
to play. The **Man Hong Kong
International Literary Festival**
(www.festival.org.hk) is one of the
biggest literary events in Asia
(though sadly it's still not all that
big). Novelists, short story writers,

and poets from around the world
give talks and readings. During the
one-night only **Hong Kong Art-
Walk** (☎ 852/2854-1018; www.hong
kongartwalk.com), more than 40
galleries are open to the public, and
many serve wine and food. In March
and April the **Ching Ming Festival**
(☎ 852/2508-1234; www.discover
hongkong.com) is a time to honor
the dead—people head to their
ancestors' graves for an annual
cleaning and for traditional picnics.
The **Hong Kong International
Film Festival** (☎ 852/2970-3300;
www.hkiff.org.hk) is held in April and
lures a plethora of local and international films (and film stars) to the
city. The **Birthday of Tin Hau,** also
in April, honors the patroness of
sailors and fisherfolk at the many Tin
Hau temples in Hong Kong (☎ 852/
2508-1234; www.discoverhonkkong.
com). The **Cheung Chau Bun Festival** is held in late April or early May
on Cheung Chau, and involves a
race for steamed buns up a tall
tower (☎ 852/2508-1234; www.
discoverhonkkong.com). The **Birthday of Lord Buddha** takes place in
May, and though you won't see too
many signs of it, you can go to the
Big Buddha on Lantau and other
spots to take part in festivities
(☎ 852/2508-1234; www.discover
hongkong.com).

SUMMER. In June you can see (and
even join) teams racing long
"dragon boats" in the waters around
Hong Kong during the **Dragon Boat
Races,** which are part of the **Tuen
Ng Festival** (☎ 852/2508-1234;
www.discoverhongkong.com). The
final race is held in Stanley. During
the **Yue Lan Festival**—the Festival
of the Hungry Ghost—in June, you'll

Previous page: Neon signs along Hong Kong's high-end shopping street, Nathan Road.

see people burning paper money and votives in the shapes of things like cars and houses. These offerings are to appease restless spirits, who are said to be allowed to walk the earth during this 2-week-long event (☎ 852/2508-1234; www.discoverhongkong.com). If you're around in July, you can check out **Hong Kong Fashion Week** (☎ 852/1830-668; www.hkfashionweekss.tdctrade.com), which involves fashion shows, among other things.

FALL. In late September and early October, the **Mid-Autumn Festival** (www.discoverhongkong.com) celebrates Hong Kong's harvest and the brightest moon of the year. It's tradition to light (or turn on battery charged) lanterns of all shapes and sizes, and sweet "moon" cakes are served (☎ 852/2508-1234; www.discoverhongkong.com). The **Chung Yueng Festival** (☎ 852/2508-1234; www.discoverhongkong.com) is the second time of the year when ancestral graves are swept and offerings are made to dead relatives. Some people celebrate by hiking in the hills, in honor of a Han dynasty story about a man who was warned by an oracle to take his family to a high place to escape a plague.

WINTER. **Chinese New Year** is the most important holiday on the calendar here. Be aware that many shops close, as people head off to spend time with their families. But there are parades and lots of Chinese fireworks. The date is set by the lunar calendar and lands in late January or early February. The **Hong Kong Arts Festival** (☎ 852/2824-2430; www.hk.artfestival.org) is 3 weeks of music, performing arts, and exhibitions from local and international artists. It's held in February and March.

The Weather

Spring and fall are mild and pleasant in Hong Kong. Summers, on the other hand, are oppressively humid (the ubiquitous air-conditioning helps make it bearable) and punctuated by occasional deluges of rain. Winters are actually very pleasant, and if you're from a cold climate, you can laugh at the very large parkas and scarves people wear in what is essentially sweater weather.

Useful Websites

- **www.centamap.com**: Detailed map showing you any destination you plug in (the "English" tab is on the left side of the page).

- **http://www.discoverhongkong.com/www.discoverhongkong.com**: This is the best resource for travelers headed to Hong Kong, and for those considering the city as a destination, with maps, major attractions, a calendar of events, hotels, restaurants, tours, and even definitions of Chinese terms and holidays.

HONG KONG'S AVERAGE DAILY TEMPERATURE & RAINFALL

	JAN	FEB	MAR	APR	MAY	JUNE
Temp. (°F)	61	61	64	72	77	80
Temp. (°C)	16	16	18	22	25	27
Rainfall (in.)	5.6	8.9	10.1	11.1	14.9	14.2

	JULY	AUG	SEPT	OCT	NOV	DEC
Temp. (°F)	84	84	80	77	70	64
Temp. (°C)	29	29	27	25	21	18
Rainfall (in.)	17.5	17.3	14.4	8.6	5.9	3.9

- **www.epd-asg.gov.hk/eindex. php**: This is the Environmental Protection Department's pollution index—sadly worth checking out in a city where the poor air quality is an issue.

- **www.hkoutdoors.com**: The most comprehensive site if you plan on doing a bit of hiking or trail running on your trip.

- **www.pccw.com/eng**: A directory of any phone numbers you might need while you're in Hong Kong.

- **www.weather.org.hk**: Check this site to see the local weather.

Cellphones (Mobile Phones)
If your phone is on a **GSM (Global System for Mobiles) Wireless Network** (GSM 900, PCS 1800, or CDMA) you will be able to make and receive calls in Hong Kong.

A cheaper option, however, is to buy a computer memory phone chip (called a SIM card) which allows you to make calls at local rates. **CSL** (852/2888-1010; www.hkcsl.com) is a local company that sells prepaid

SIM cards for as little as $HK88. They also rent phones for $HK35 per day, with rechargeable SIM chips costing $HK180 to $HK280 for 293 to 600 minutes. Top-up cards cost $HK100 to $HK500. Other places that sell SIM cards and rent phones include **SmarTone** (852/2880-2688; www.smartone-vodafone.com), and **3 Hong Kong** (852/3162-8888; www.three.com.hk), which both have shops all over town.

Car Rentals
There's no need to rent a car, given that Hong Kong is a small city with a multitude of transportation options, and parking can be a hassle. But if you want or need to have a car at your disposal, book one before you leave home—and remember that companies often offer better rates if you book online. Try **Hertz** (www. hertz.com) or **Avis** (www.avis. com.hk).

If you want to be driven around at your whim, you can hire a car with a driver from **Ace Hire Car** (www.acehirecar.com.hk).

Getting **There**

By Plane
Hong Kong International Airport is consistently ranked one of the best airports in the world (852/ 2181-8888; www.hongkongairport. com). If you want a nonstop flight, book early, though nonstops are often pricier that those that stop in places like Taiwan or Tokyo. Some major airlines flying to Hong Kong from North America, Europe, and Australia include **Air Canada** (888/247-2262; www.aircanada.com); **British Airways** (0870/850-9850; www. britishairways.com); **Cathay Pacific Airways** (800/233-2742;

www.cathaypacific.com), Hong Kong's own airline with great service and comfort; **Continental Airlines** (800/231-0856; www.continental. com); **Qantas** (02/9691-3636; www.qantas.com); and **Singapore Airlines** (800/742-3333; www. singaporeair.com).

From Hong Kong International Airport: Once you collect your baggage and enter the arrival hall, you'll have a chance to withdraw money from international ATMs, get food, and collect maps and tourist information from the Hong Kong Tourism Board booths.

Once you're set, there are a number of ways to get into the city. The quickest and easiest is the **Airport Express Line** (852/2881-8888; www.mtr.com.hk). This high-speed train stops in Tsim Sha Tsui and Hong Kong Island Central and costs around $HK100. Trains run every 12 minutes between 6am and 1am and it takes 24 minutes to get to the center of the city. On your way back to the airport, you can even get your boarding pass and check your luggage at the train terminal. Free shuttle buses take passengers to and from most major hotels (see www.mtr.com.hk for a list of which hotels are served).

A slightly cheaper way to get into the city is **Citflyer Airbuses** (852/2873-0818; www.citybus.com.hk). Airbus A21 goes through Mong Kok, Yau Ma Tei, Jordan, and down Nathan Road through Tsim Sha Tsui; the A11 goes to Hong Kong Island. Buses depart every 10 to 30 minutes for $HK33 to Kowloon and $HK40 to the island.

The easiest and consequently priciest choice is to take a **taxi.** Depending on where you're going, a cab can cost around $HK400 once the baggage fee is added in. It takes about 30 to 45 minutes to get to Central.

By Train

Crossing into Hong Kong from China is easiest on the **Kowloon-Canton Railway's East Rail,** which starts on the Hong Kong side in Lo Wu and stops at Hung Hom and East Tsim Sha Tsui. The price is $HK66 for first class and $HK33 for second class.

The **Kowloon-Guangzhou Express Train** (www.kcrc.com) leaves daily; the fare is $HK180 and takes just under 2 hours. Tickets can be booked through the China Travel Service or by calling the Intercity Passenger Service Hotline (852/2947-7888).

Another rail links Kowloon with Shanghai and Beijing. Trains from Beijing cost $HK547/$HK934 for hard sleeper/soft sleeper and from Shanghai for $HK508/$HK825 for hard sleeper/soft sleeper. Both take around 24 hours.

By Bus

A number of bus companies offer routes to and from Guangzhou and Shenzhen at competitive rates. Some options are **CTS Express Coach** (852/2365-0118; ctsbus.hkcts.com), **Eternal East** (852/3412-6677; www.eebus.com), **Gogobus** (852/2375-0099; www.gogobus.com), **Motor Transport Company of Guangdong & Hong Kong** (852/2735-2991; www.gdhkmtc.com).

Boat

Boats leave from Guangdong, Shenzhen, and Macau on a regular basis. Carriers **TurboJET** (852/2859-3333; www.turbojet.com.hk) and **New World First Ferry** (852/2131-8181; www.nwff.com.hk) serve all three regions.

Getting **Around**

By Train

The **Mass Transit Railway (MTR)** (852/2881-8888; www.mtr.com.hk) is the fastest way to get around the city, though it often requires some long walks both under and above ground. (In this guidebook, we often cite the MTR as a way to get to destinations, but if you're in a rush I recommend taking a taxi.) You can buy tickets to your exact destination at machines in the terminal of any MTR station; tickets range from $HK4 to $HK26. You can also get an Octopus card that you can swipe to get on and off, and each time you use it, you'll get a readout of how much money you have left on the card. These prepaid cards also work for buses, ferries, and at chosen places around the city (such as grocery stores and movie theaters).

The MTR's blue line runs along Hong Kong Island; the orange line runs from the island to Kowloon and Disneyland; the red line runs from the island to Kowloon and the west; the purple line runs from the island to Kowloon and the east; and the green line runs on Kowloon to the east. The Airport Express line goes to Lantau and the airport and connects with the orange line at some stops.

The **Kowloon-Canton Railway** (KCR; ☎ 852/2929-3399; www.kcrc. com) has two lines and is useful for reaching destinations in the New Territories. The KCR East Rail runs from East Tsim Sha Tsui to Low Wu and the mainland border. The KCR West Rail links Nam Cheong station in Sham Shui Po with Tuen Mun in the New Territories.

Hong Kong's **double-decker trams** are yet another option. This mode of transport is slow, but fun and cheap—a ride costs $HK2. Trams operate from 6am to 12:30am and cover six routes around the island. They are: Kennedy Town to Western Market, Kennedy Town to Causeway Bay, Kennedy Town to Happy Valley, Sai Ying Pun (Whitty St.) to North Point, Sheung Wan (Western Market) to Shau Kei Wan, and Happy Valley to Shau Kei Wan.

By Bus

Hong Kong's **Citybus** (www.citybus. com.hk) is fairly easy to use if you have a map and a little patience. It can also be worthwhile as it can take you just about everywhere in Hong

Kong all hours of the day at cheap rates. Bus fares range from $HK2.40 to $HK45 depending on where you're going and at what time of day. Central's bus station below Exchange Square is a convenient station, leading to Aberdeen, Repulse Bay, and Stanley. In Kowloon, the CTS bus terminals are located at or near either end of the Star Ferry pier. To figure out where buses go, just follow their routes on signs at bus stops. All buses with an M stop at MTR stations and those with an X are express and sometimes take the highways, so be careful you don't overshoot your stop if taking them.

Minibuses, or "public light buses," also cover the entirety of Hong Kong. These are harder for visitors to get the hang of, but you can figure out where they go by asking locals for help. Small red minibuses ($HK2–$HK20) don't run according to chosen stops and you can hop off by calling out your desired stop to the driver. The green "maxicabs" run set routes and make designated stops. The 1, for instance, runs from next to Hong Kong station to Victoria Peak for $HK8.

By Ferry

There are four **Star Ferry** (www. starferry.com.hk) routes between the island and the peninsula. The routes run from Central to Tsim Sha Tsui, Central to Hung Hom, and Wan Chai to Tsim Sha Tsui and Hung Hom. A number of other ferries go to outlying islands like Lantau, Cheung Chau, and Lamma. You can catch these ferries at the Central ferry pier.

By Car

Driving is not recommended because taxis are cheap and destinations are close together. Frequent traffic jams are also a deterrent. If you do drive, use **www.centamap.com** to find your way, then get a Hong Kong street map when you're in the city.

Fast **Facts**

APARTMENT RENTALS There are a number of serviced apartments available for long-term stays in Hong Kong. They range from the very expensive to the reasonably inexpensive. **Four Seasons Place Hong Kong** (☎ 852/3196-8228; www.fsphk.com) is on the former end, **W Studios** (☎ 852/9866-8333; www.wstudios.com.hk) on the latter. Check this website for a list: http://hongkong.asiaxpat.com/property/serviced.asp.

ATMS/CASHPOINTS You can withdraw funds from home checking and savings accounts if you have a card that's part of the **Cirrus** or **PLUS** network. There are many ATMs scattered around the city. Most banks charge a fee for international withdrawals, so check before you leave home.

BABYSITTING A reliable place to get part-time sitters or longer-term nannies is **The Nanny Experts** (☎ 852/2335-1127; www.the nannyexperts.com).

BIKE RENTALS I wouldn't bother renting bikes to cruise around Hong Kong, with its crowded sidewalks and winding roads. But it's a good idea to rent bikes during day trips, such as on Cheung Chau, Lantau, and at Tai Mei Tek in the New Territories. Small shops are available and easy to find in all three areas.

BUSINESS HOURS Business hours are generally 9am to 5:30 or 6pm Monday to Friday and 9am to 12pm on Saturday. Some offices close for lunch from 1 to 2pm. Most banks, post offices, shops, and attractions are closed on public holidays.

CONSULATES & EMBASSIES **American Consulate,** 26 Garden Rd., Central (☎ 852/2523-9011; www.hongkong.usconsulate.gov);

Canadian Consulate, 11th–14th Floor of Tower One, Exchange Square, 8 Connaught Place, Central (☎ 852/2867-7348; www.dfait-maeci.gc.ca/asia/hongkong); **British Consulate,** 1 Supreme Rd., Central (☎ 852/2901-3000; www.british consulate.org.hk); **Australian Consulate,** 23rd Floor Harbour Centre, 25 Harbour Rd., Wan Chai (☎ 852/2525-5044; www.hongkong.china. embassy.gov.au).

CREDIT CARDS Most major credit cards are accepted in large shops, restaurants, hotels, and ticket booths. You're best bet is to have a Visa, MasterCard, or American Express, though often Diners Club and JCB are taken. Bring your banking and credit card details in case you need to call to cancel anything or have trouble withdrawing funds.

CURRENCY EXCHANGE You can cash traveler's checks or exchange money at banks or foreign exchange offices around the city, including those in hotels and at the airport.

CUSTOMS When entering Hong Kong, those18 and older can bring in duty free a 1-liter (34-oz.) bottle of alcohol and 200 cigarettes, 50 cigars, or 250 grams of tobacco. To see what you can take home, check the website of your country's Customs and border protection department.

DENTISTS & DOCTORS There are 41 public hospitals in Hong Kong. Two reliable options are **Queen Mary Hospital,** 102 Pokfulam Rd. (☎ 852/2855-3838), and **Queen Elizabeth Hospital,** 30 Gascoigne Rd. (☎ 852/2958-8888). Most first-class hotels in Hong Kong actually have in-house medical clinics with registered nurses and doctors on call in case of emergencies. The U.S. consulate also provides a list of English-speaking doctors.

ELECTRICITY The standard voltage is 220 volts, 50 hertz alternating current. Most outlets are designed to accommodate the British three square pins. Buy an adapter before you leave home or pick one up at a shop in the Hong Kong airport terminal or around the city.

EMERGENCIES To call for an ambulance or the police, or in case of a fire, dial ☎ **999.**

EVENT LISTINGS *HK Magazine*, *BC Magazine*, and local newspapers all list events in the city. Websites like **www.discoverhongkong.com** also have event calendars.

FAMILY TRAVEL Hong Kong is a great place to travel with older children, since there's so much to see and do (and there's Ocean Park and Hong Kong Disneyland). There are also many discounts available for kids for everything from shows to public transportation. Traveling with small kids is a bit trickier, since many places are crowded and noisy. If you're traveling with an infant or toddler, be prepared for lots of tight spaces and steep steps—your stroller may not fit.

GAY & LESBIAN TRAVELERS There is a vibrant, if not readily apparent, gay and lesbian community in Hong Kong. Discrimination is not a serious issue here, though, as in most places, you may encounter some less-than-open-minded types. There are a limited number of gay bars and clubs, many places have designated gay or lesbian nights. Check out *Gmagazine*, a small monthly magazine distributed in clubs, bars, and other venues for event listings.

HOLIDAYS The dates of many public holidays change from year to year, based on the lunar calendar. Check out www.gov.hk/en/about/abouthk/holiday/index.htm for details. In general, public holidays are: New Year's Day on January 1, Lunar New Year in February, Ching Ming Festival in April, Labour Day and Buddha's Birthday, both in May, Tuen Ng Festival in June, Establishment Day of the Special Administrative Region on July 2, the day following the Mid-Autumn Festival in September, National Day on October 1, Chung Yeung Festival in October, Christmas on December 25, and Boxing Day on December 26.

INSURANCE Although Hong Kong is a safe travel destination, if you want to insure your tickets, belongings, or health, go to **InsureMyTrip.com** for estimates on travel insurance. For trip cancellation insurance, try **Travel Guard International** (☎ **800/826-4919;** www.travelguard.com). For medical insurance, **Travel Assistance International** (☎ **800/821-2828;** www.travelassistance.com) offers plans that cover you while you're on the road. For lost-luggage insurance, check with your airline.

INTERNET ACCESS Wireless access is available for a fee in the Hong Kong International Airport and in most major hotels. If you simply want to browse or check e-mail, go to any of the **Pacific Coffee Company** (www.pacificcoffee.com) shops around the city and you can surf for free if you buy something. You can also get online for free, but with a bit of a wait, at the **Central Library** in Causeway Bay (66 Causeway Rd.; ☎ **852/3150-1234;** www.hkpl.gov.hk). Internet cafes are also easy to find throughout the city.

LIQUOR LAWS The drinking (and smoking) age in Hong Kong is 18. Beer and wine can be found at convenience stores around the city, and liquor is also sold at department stores and supermarkets. Bar hours vary, but some stay open until dawn.

LOST PROPERTY To report lost or stolen property, call the police at ☎ **852/2527-7177.** Information on police stations is available at www.police.gov.hk.

MAIL Postal service in Hong Kong is safe and reliable, and most post offices are open Monday to Friday from 9:30am to 5pm and Saturday from 9:30am to 1pm. Postal workers generally speak some English, so you shouldn't have trouble getting the correct stamps and postage fees. Airmail letters take about 5 to 7 days to reach their destination in the U.S. and Europe. The main post office is on Hong Kong Island (2 Connaught Place, Central; ☎ 852/2921-2222). For other locations check out www.hongkongpost.com.

MONEY The local currency is the Hong Kong dollar ($HK), which is pegged to the U.S. dollar at a rate of around US$1 to $HK7.80. The HK dollar is divided into denominations of $10, $20, $50, $100, $500, and $1,000. There are coins of 10 cents, 20 cents, 50 cents, $1, $2, $5, and $10.

NEWSPAPERS & MAGAZINES The best local English-language newspaper is the *South China Morning Post* (www.scmp.com), which comes out daily and sells for $HK7. The *Hong Kong Standard* (www.thestandard.com.hk) focuses on business and comes out Monday to Saturday and costs $HK6. The *China Daily* is a state-run newspaper out of Beijing that brings news from the mainland as well as reports on Hong Kong from a mainland perspective; it sells for $HK6.

There are also a number of local magazines, such as the *Hong Kong Tatler* (www.hktatler.com) and publications on business and the economy. International titles are readily available in airports, hotels, and bookstores, and include the *Wall Street Journal Asia*, *USA Today*, the *International Herald Tribune* (owned by the *New York Times* and running

much of its international news), the *Financial Times*, and *Time Asia*.

PASSES You can buy a pass that will grant you entry to all of Hong Kong's museums. Prices vary, so check for details at www.discoverhongkong.com. A prepaid Octopus card, available at all MTR stations, will allow you to swipe on and off all major public transportation and can be used like a debit card at many shops and venues around the city.

PASSPORTS If your passport is lost or stolen, contact your consulate or embassy. It's smart to have photocopies of all your important documents such as your passport and credit cards with you, just in case they go missing.

PHARMACIES There are no 24-hour drugstores in Hong Kong, so if you're in desperate need of a prescription, contact a hospital or the police. One of the best-known pharmacies is Watson's—there are more than 100 around the city and they're open from 9am to 10pm daily. You can also buy medication at small Chinese drugstores.

POLICE Dial ☎ 999 in an emergency. Otherwise, you can call the police via a crime hotline at ☎ 852/2527-7177. The Rape Crisis Line is ☎ 852/2375-5322.

RESTROOMS There are public toilets all around Hong Kong that are free of charge. Most are fairly clean, with Western-style toilets. Still, I highly suggest carrying your own tissues around with you. Be warned that there are no public bathrooms in the MTR network.

SAFETY Hong Kong is a very safe city for tourists. But like any city, you should keep your wits about you, protect your belongings, and not wander around in the middle of the night with no clue where you're going. There have been very rare cases of hikers being robbed, though there's a greater chance of heat stroke for those who don't dress appropriately and carry enough water.

SENIOR TRAVELERS Seniors receive discounts to many museums, shows, public transportation options, and activities in Hong Kong; bring along identification that clearly states your age. Some discounts are available for those 60 and over, while others are only open to those 65 and over, so be sure to ask. Be aware that many activities in Hong Kong involve walking—though with a little extra planning, you can minimize how much time you spend on your feet. Also, the heat in the summer can be stifling, an issue for both the young and aged.

SMOKING You can still smoke in many of Hong Kong's bars and restaurants, though rules are slowly being established to put an end to this. There are generally nonsmoking rooms available in hotels and nonsmoking seating in large restaurants. Smoking is banned in cinemas, shopping malls, supermarkets, department stores, and banks.

STAYING HEALTHY The two biggest concerns for health in Hong Kong in the past decade have been **bird flu** and **SARS**. The former has been contained, though it doesn't hurt to read up on it before coming to Hong Kong and while in the city. The latter has shown no signs of returning since the last outbreak in 2003. Otherwise, Hong Kong is as safe for a short stay as any developed country (though in the long-term, the air pollution may be detrimental to your health). Generally, you can dine without worry anywhere in the city, including roadside eateries, although it's always wise to use caution when ordering seafood. If you're worried that it isn't fresh, skip it. It's safe to drink water in the city center, including ice in restaurants.

But if you're traveling in the rural areas of Hong Kong or in mainland China, definitely stick with bottled water.

TAXES Hotels will add a 10% service charge and a 3% government tax to your bill. Restaurants and bars will add a 10% service charge, but there is no tax. There's an airport departure tax of \$HK120 that will generally be included in your ticket price. There is no tax for purchasing electronics, which is why buying those items here is often such a steal.

TELEPHONES The international country code for Hong Kong is 852. All local calls in Hong Kong are free except at public pay phones, where they cost \$HK1 for every 5 minutes. International direct-dial (IDD) calls can be made from public phones with a phone card or from hotels. Phone cards are sold at 7-Elevens, Circle Ks, and other convenience stores around the city. To make **international calls** from Hong Kong dial ☎ 001 and then the country code (**U.S.** or **Canada** 1; **UK** 44; **Ireland** 353; **Australia** 61; **New Zealand** 64). For **directory assistance in English** call ☎ 1081.

TELEVISION & RADIO The two English-language stations in Hong Kong are TVB Pearl and ATV World. English-language radio includes RTHK Radio 3 (567AM, 1584AM, 97.9FM, and 106.8FM). RTHK Radio 4 (97.6FM–98.9FM), RTHK Radio 6 (675AM), AM 864 (864AM), and Metro Plus (1044AM).

TICKETS You can get tickets at any of the 34 URBTIX outlets around the city or online at http://urbtix.city line.com.hk.

TIME Hong Kong standard time is 8 hours ahead of Greenwich Mean Time; there is no daylight saving time.

TIPPING Hong Kong is a place of relatively small tips. Cab drivers only expect you to round up to the nearest dollar, and hotel staff will be happy with \$HK10 to \$HK20. Most restaurants and some bars add a 10% service charge, so doing 5% to 10% on top of that is acceptable.

TOURIST OFFICES The **Hong Kong Tourism Board** (☎ 852/2508-1234; www.discoverhongkong.com) comes up a lot in this book because it provides helpful ways to get information and ideas for your vacation. There are branches at the Hong Kong International Airport, the Star Ferry Concourse in Tsim Sha Tsui, and the MTR Station in Causeway Bay near exit F.

TOURS There are tons of tours available in Hong Kong. Some of the better ones are from the **Hong Kong Tourist Board** (☎ 852/2508-1234; www.discoverhongkong.com) and **Splendid Tours & Travel** (☎ 852/2316-2151; www.splendidtours.com). You can go go dolphin spotting with **Hong Kong Dolphinwatch** (☎ 852/2984-1414; www.hkdolphinwatch.com), and go outdoors with **Kayak and Hike** (☎ 852/9300-5197; www.kayak-and-hike.com). Otherwise, **Sky Bird Travel** (☎ 852/2369-9628; www.skybird.com.hk) offers cultural tours highlighting Chinese traditions, and **Walk the Talk** (☎ 852/2380-7756; www.walkthetalk.hk) provides a useful audio guide to major attractions that uses your mobile phone and is available in Hong Kong Tourism Board branches and some bookshops.

TRAVELERS WITH DISABILITIES Hong Kong tries, but often fails, to be a friendly city to those with disabilities. If you're planning a trip, be aware that while MTR stops have escalators and elevators, there are often very long distances in between the entrances and exits and the train; there are also generally massive crowds to contend with. Many buses are now wheelchair accessible, though English may be a problem with some bus drivers. Taxis are generally easy to find in any major part of the city, and most buildings have elevators. Public toilets are generally wheelchair accessible, and crosswalks are equipped with sound sensors for crossing and there are textured lines on major streets for the visually impaired. For information contact the **Transport Department** (☎ 852/2804-2660; www.td.gov.hk) or the **Joint Council for the Physically and Mentally Disabled** (☎ 852/2864-2931; Room 1204, 12th Floor, Duke of Windsor Social Service Building, 15 Hennessy Rd., Wan Chai).

VISAS Citizens of Australia, Canada, Japan, New Zealand, and the USA can enter Hong Kong for 90 days without a visa. People from South Africa have 30 days, and people from the U.K. and other European Union countries have 180 days. If coming from other countries, please check visa regulations at www.immd.gov.hk/ehtml/hkvisas_4.htm. If you're traveling on to mainland China, you will need a visa and should plan in advance as it is occasionally a difficult process. You can do so fairly easily with China Travel Service (www.ctshk.com).

Hong Kong: **A Brief History**

4000–1500 B.C. Early settlers of Asian Mongoloid background settle throughout southern China,

including Hong Kong. They leave behind tools and burial grounds.

221–206 B.C. Hong Kong is incorporated into China under the Qin dynasty.

A.D. 618–907 Under the Tang dynasty, the Guangdong region becomes a major trading center. Tuen Mun, in what is known as Hong Kong's New Territories, was a naval base, salt production center, and base for pearl trading.

960–1500S Pirates roam the seas around Hong Kong.

1276 During the Mongol invasion, the Southern Song dynasty court moved to Lantau Island, and then to Kowloon City. Hong Kong also saw its first population boom thanks to Chinese refugees during this period.

1514 Portuguese traders establish a base in Hong Kong.

1839 The Chinese emperor destroys the British opium stockpile in a desperate attempt to quell the growing opium trade, which is draining China's wealth. The British Royal Navy retaliates by firing on Chinese war junks, starting the First Opium War.

1842 The Treaty of Nanking is signed by China and Britain, putting an end to the First Opium War. The treaty cedes Hong Kong Island to Britain. Sir Henry Pottinger is the territory's first governor.

1860 Under the Peking Convention of 1860, following the Second Opium War, China cedes the Kowloon area to Britain.

1865 The Hongkong and Shanghai Banking Corporation (HSBC) is founded.

1888 The Peak Tram makes its first run up Victoria Peak, reducing the travel time from 3 hours to 8 minutes.

1898 Under the Second Peking Convention, Britain and China agree on a 99-year lease on the New Territories, including surrounding islands. The British, who fear Hong Kong will be vulnerable to Chinese attack without the added land, pay nothing. Had the British not settled on a lease, it's possible they would not have had to hand Hong Kong back to China in 1997. The first major wave of Chinese immigrants arrives in Hong Kong, fleeing civil war.

1900 Hong Kong's population is 263,000.

1912 The University of Hong Kong opens.

1904 The tram system is constructed along the waterfront on Hong Kong Island.

1910 The Kowloon Railway is completed, linking Hong Kong with China.

1911 The Manchu dynasty is overthrown by Sun Yat-sen's Nationalist revolution, and a second wave of Chinese refugees arrives in Hong Kong.

1925 Hong Kong's first and only general strike occurs. Nationalists and Communists join in a united front, organizing antiforeign strikes and boycotts in China that spread to Hong Kong. The economy is paralyzed.

1941–45 Japan invades and occupies Hong Kong during World War II. After the war ended in 1945, Britain resumed control of Hong Kong.

1949 China's Communists defeat the Nationalists and win control of China. The war drives many to Hong Kong, where squatter villages begin to develop on the city's outskirts.

1960–70S Hong Kong residents begin to clash with the colonial government and police, some under the rubric of Communism akin to that on the mainland. Officials in Hong Kong step up anti-Communist purges and close pro-Beijing newspapers. But as the city's economy takes off thanks to manufacturing and international trade, economics wins out over rebellion.

1976 Mao Zedong, China's Communist chairman, dies and Deng Xiaoping emerges as the country's leader, calling for opening and reform. Britain asks for a renewal on its 99-year lease of the New Territories, but Deng refuses and calls for the return of all of Hong Kong to China.

1979 The MTR transportation system is founded.

1984 British prime minister Margaret Thatcher and China's premiere, Zhao Ziyang, sign the Joint Declaration requiring Britain to transfer sovereignty of Hong Kong to China at midnight on June 30, 1997. China vows to give Hong Kong a "high degree of autonomy" and permits it to retain its capitalist system for 50 years after 1997.

1989 After Beijing's military crackdown on protestors in Tiananmen Square, more than one million people in Hong Kong take to the streets in protest.

1992–95 The British governor, Christopher Patten, announces democratic reforms for the 1994 local and 1995 legislative elections. Critics see it as a last effort to bring democracy to Hong Kong after years of colonial rule. Relations between China and Britain grow strained, and many

Hong Kong residents apply for British and Canadian citizenship.

JULY 1, 1997 Hong Kong is officially ceded to China and becomes a Special Autonomous Region (SAR). Beijing strikes down many of the last minute rules and liberties Patten put in place before he left, and institutes an interim legislature. Port tycoon Tung Chee-hwa, viewed by many as Beijing's handpicked choice, becomes chief executive of the SAR.

OCTOBER 23, 1997 The Hong Kong stock market crashes after interest rates are raised to protect the Hong Kong dollar from currency speculators. Millions of dollars are lost overnight and the property market goes into a slump.

1998 The SAR has its first legislative election under Chinese rule. Pro-democracy politicians win 60% of the popular vote but only 20 seats in the 60-seat legislature. In the first major protest since Tiananmen Square in 1989, 40,000 people commemorate the anniversary of that incident. Hong Kong International Airport opens.

FEBRUARY 19, 2002 Hong Kong's chief executive, Tung Chee-hwa, secures a second 5-year term in office without an election.

JUNE 24, 2002 Tung announces a new cabinet of ministers that marks the biggest shake-up in the territory's governance since it ceased to be a colony.

2003 Severe Acute Respiratory Syndrome (SARS) rocks the territory and bruises the economy.

JUNE 21, 2005 Donald Tsang takes over as chief executive of Hong Kong after the resignation of Tung Chee-hwa, who had been criticized by the public for bungling leadership of the territory.

The **People**

Hong Kong is a city of 6.8 million people on a land area of approximately 1,100 sq. km (425 sq. miles, or half the size of Rhode Island in the U.S.). Though its British past makes it like no other city in China, it's still 95% ethnically Chinese, with over half of these residents born in Hong Kong.

Most Chinese in Hong Kong come from southern China, thus the establishment of Cantonese instead of Mandarin as the local language. Others are Hakka, traditionally a farming people, and Tanka, who make up the majority of Hong Kong's dwindling boat-dwelling fishers.

Influence from other parts of China is becoming more and more evident, however, in architecture, national issues, and even cuisine, as more and more Sichuan, Pekingese, and Shanghainese restaurants spring up. Long a beacon of money and upward mobility to mainland Chinese, people still flock to Hong Kong if they can afford it and can find work. About 54,000 mainland Chinese come to try to make it in Hong Kong every year.

Because of its dense population, limited land space, and 16,000 people per square mile, Hong Kong has long been plagued with housing shortages. In 1953, a huge fire left more than 50,000 people homeless. Since then, Hong Kong has implemented a housing scheme to try and provide every family with a home.

By 1993, more than half of Hong Kong's population lived in government-subsidized public housing. A typical apartment in such living areas is about 23 sq. m (250 sq. ft.), with a single window. It has a living room/bedroom, small cooking area, and bathroom and is often shared by a couple with one or two children. While space may be tight, the standards of living are decent. According to the government, every household in Hong Kong has at least one television, more than enough food, and access to public transportation and recreation in public facilities.

Useful Phrases & Menu Terms

Cantonese and English are Hong Kong's two official languages, with Cantonese being used by some 94% of the population. Despite this fact, most people in Hong Kong speak English, so you should have no problem getting around. Many people also speak Mandarin, the Chinese language used on most of the mainland, along with many other local dialects. It's helpful, however, to know some basic words and their meanings. Cantonese is a difficult language for native-English speakers because it has nine different tones, though you can make do with six. This means that a word pronounced "yow," depending on the tone, can mean thin, have, friend, to worry, or to rest. To complicate matters further, English speakers learn the language through pinyin, while Chinese speakers read characters. If you really want to learn Chinese, I recommend attending classes or hiring a tutor—it's difficult for books to convey how to pronounce tone. But for now, just trying some of these words will endear you to locals and get you, at worst, an uncomprehending smile.

Accommodations

ENGLISH	CANTONESE
I'm looking for . . .	Ngo yiu wan . . .
Guesthouse	Jiu doi so
Hotel	Jau dim
Do you have any rooms available?	Yau mo fong a?
I'd like a (single/double) room.	Ngo seung yiu yat gaan (daan yan/seung yan) fong.
How much is it per night?	Yiu gei do cin yat maan a?

Shopping

ENGLISH	CANTONESE
How much does this cost?	Ni go gei do chin a?
That's too much.	Taai gwai loa.
I want to buy . . .	Ngo seung maai . . .
Do you accept credit cards?	Nei dei sau m sau sun yung kaat a?
I'm just looking.	Ngo sin tai yat tai.
More	Do di
Less	Siu di
Bigger	Daai di
Smaller	Sai di

Greetings

ENGLISH	CANTONESE
Hello, how are you?	Nei ho ma?
Goodbye.	Baai baai/joi gin.
Yes	Hai
No	M hai
I'm fine.	Ngo gei ho.
Excuse me.	M goi.
Thank you (for a gift).	Do je.
Thank you (for service).	M goi.
Do you speak English?	Nei sik m sik gong ying man a?
I don't understand.	Ngo m ming.
What's your surname?	Cheng man gwai sing?
My surname is . . .	Siu sing . . .
My name is . . .	Ngo giu . . .
Can you please repeat that?	Cheng joi gong yat chi?

Emergencies

ENGLISH	CANTONESE
I'm sick.	Ngo yau beng.
Call the police!	Giu ging chaat!
Call an ambulance!	Giu gau seung che!

Call a doctor!	Giu yi sang!
Help!	Gau meng a!
Where's the police station?	Ging chue hai bin do a?

Health

ENGLISH	CANTONESE
Where's the nearest . . . , please?	Cheng man jui kan ge . . . bin do a?
Chemist/pharmacy	Yeuk fong
Doctor	Yi sang
Dentist	Nga yi sang
Hospital	Yi yuen
I'm sick.	Ngo yau beng.
I need a doctor.	Ngo yiu tai yi sang.
Asthma	Yau haau chuen.
Diarrhea	To ngo
Fever	Yau faat siu
Headache	Tau tung
Pain	Tung

Questions

ENGLISH	CANTONESE
Who?	Bin go a?
What?	Mat ye a?
When?	Gei si a?
Where?	Bin do a?
How?	Dim Yeung a?

Restaurants & Food

ENGLISH	CANTONESE
Bring the check please.	M goi, maai daan.
I'm a vegetarian.	Ngo hai sik jaai ge.
That was delicious.	Jan ho mei.
Breakfast	Jo chaan
Dim sum	Dim sam
Lunch	Ng chaan
Dinner	Maan chaan
Can you recommend a . . . ?	Ho m ho yi gai siu gaan . . . ?
Bar	Jau ba
Restaurant	Chaan teng
Roast pork	Char siu
Barbecued pork with rice	Char siu fan
Roast duck	Char siu ngap
Fried rice	Chau fan
Fried noodles	Chau min
Braised mixed vegetables	Lo hong tsai

Time

ENGLISH	CANTONESE
Today	Gam yat
Tomorrow	Ting yat
Yesterday	Kam yat

Monday	Sing kei yat
Tuesday	Sing kei yi
Wednesday	Sing kei saam
Thursday	Sing kei sei
Friday	Sing kei ng
Saturday	Sing kei luk
Sunday	Sing kei yat

Numbers

ENGLISH	CANTONESE
0	Ling
1	Yat
2	Yi (Leung for pair)
3	Saam
4	Sei
5	Ng
6	Luk
7	Chat
8	Baat
9	Gau
10	Sap
11	Sap yat
12	Sap yi
20	Yi sap
30	Saam sap
40	Sei sap
50	Ng sap
100	Yat baak
1,000	Yat chin

Toll-Free Numbers & Websites

From the U.S. & Canada

AIR CANADA
☎ 888/247-2262
www.aircanada.com

CATHAY PACIFIC AIRWAYS
☎ 800/233-2742
www.cathaypacific.com

CONTINENTAL AIRLINES
☎ 800/231-0856
www.continental.com

JAPAN AIRLINES
☎ 800/525-3663
www.japanair.com

KOREAN AIR
☎ 800/438-5000
www.koreanair.com

NORTHWEST AIRLINES
☎ 800/447-4747
www.nwa.com

PHILIPPINE AIRLINES
☎ 800/435-9725
www.philippineairlines.com

SINGAPORE AIRLINES
☎ 800/742-3333
www.singaporeair.com

UNITED AIRLINES
☎ 800/538-2929
www.united.com

From the U.K.
BRITISH AIRWAYS
☎ 0870/850-9850
www.britishairways.com
CATHAY PACIFIC
☎ 020/8834-8888
www.cathaypacific.com
VIRGIN ATLANTIC AIRWAYS
☎ 0870/380-2007
www.virgin-atlantic.com

From Australia
CATHAY PACIFIC
☎ 131747
www.cathaypacific.com
QANTAS
☎ 131313
www.qantas.com.au

From New Zealand
CATHAY PACIFIC
☎ 0508/800454
www.cathaypacific.com

Discount Airfare Websites:
www.orbitz.com
www.zuji.com
www.cheapflights.com
www.kayak.com
www.opodo.co.uk
www.priceline.com
www.sidestep.com

Major Hotel & Motel Chains
CROWNE PLAZA HOTELS
☎ 888/303-1746
www.ichotelsgroup.com/crowneplaza

FOUR SEASONS
☎ 800/819-5053 (in US and Canada)
☎ 0800/6488-6488 (in UK)
www.fourseasons.com
HILTON HOTELS
☎ 800/HILTONS (800/445-8667) (in US and Canada)
☎ 087/0590-9090 (in UK)
www.hilton.com
HOLIDAY INN
☎ 800/315-2621 (in US and Canada)
☎ 0800/405-060 (in UK)
www.holidayinn.com
HYATT
☎ 888/591-1234 (in US and Canada)
☎ 084/5888-1234 (in UK)
www.hyatt.com
INTERCONTINENTAL HOTELS & RESORTS
☎ 800/424-6835 (in US and Canada)
☎ 0800/1800-1800 (in UK)
www.ichotelsgroup.com
MARRIOTT
☎ 877/236-2427 (in US and Canada)
☎ 0800/221-222 (in UK)
www.marriott.com
RENAISSANCE
☎ 888/236-2427
www.renaissance.com
RITZ-CARLTON
☎ 800/241-3333
www.ritzcarlton.com

Discount Hotel Websites:
www.hotels.com
www.quickbook.com
www.travelaxe.net
www.tripadviser.com
www.asiatravel.com
www.asiahotels.com
www.planetholiday.com

Index

See also Accommodations and Restaurant indexes, below.

Photo **Credits**

Damm/eStock Photo; p 32, bottom: © travelstock 44/Alamy; p 33, top: © Peter Bowater/Alamy; p 33, bottom: © Pat Behnke/Alamy; p 36, top: © Dallas Stribley/Lonely Planet Images; p 36, bottom: © BOBBY YIP/Reuters/Corbis; p 37, top: © Derek M. Allan; Travel Ink/Corbis; p 37, bottom: © Steve Vidler/eStock Photo; p 38, top: © Reuters/CORBIS; p 38, bottom: © Greg Elms/Lonely Planet Images; p 39: © Miles Ertman/Masterfile; p 41, top: © Rough Guides/Alamy; p 41, bottom: © Ron Stroud/Masterfile; p 42, top: © Timothy O'Rourke; p 42, bottom: © Timothy O'Rourke; p 43: © Timothy O'Rourke; p 45, top: © AW Photography/Alamy; p 45, bottom: © Michele Falzone/Alamy; p 46: © Gareth Jones/Jupiterimages; p 47: © Doug Houghton/Alamy; p 49, top: © Greg Elms/Lonely Planet Images; p 49, bottom: © Lyndon Giffard/Alamy; p 50: © Timothy O'Rourke; p 51, top: © Timothy O'Rourke; p 51, middle: © Timothy O'Rourke; p 52, top: © Timothy O'Rourke; p 52, bottom: © Robert Harding Picture Library Ltd/Alamy; p 53: © Timothy O'Rourke; p 54: © Timothy O'Rourke; p 58: © Timothy O'Rourke; p 59, top: © Timothy O'Rourke; p 59, bottom: © Timothy O'Rourke; p 60, top: © Timothy O'Rourke; p 60, bottom: © Timothy O'Rourke; p 61, top: © Guillaume Jioux/AGE Fotostock; p 61, bottom: © Timothy O'Rourke; p 62, top: © Timothy O'Rourke; p 62, bottom: © Timothy O'Rourke; p 63, top: © Timothy O'Rourke; p 63, bottom: © Timothy O'Rourke; p 64, top: © Timothy O'Rourke; p 64, bottom: © Werner Otto/AGE Fotostock; p 65: © islandspics HK/Alamy; p 66: © Timothy O'Rourke; p 67: © ArkReligion.com/Alamy; p 70, top: © Robert Harding Picture Library Ltd/Alamy; p 70, bottom: © Timothy O'Rourke; p 71, top: © Timothy O'Rourke; p 71, bottom: © Dbimages/Alamy; p 74, top: © Dbimages/Alamy; p 74, bottom: © Doug Houghton; p 75: © Michael Setboun/Corbis; p 76: © James Marshall/Corbis; p 77: © Timothy O'Rourke; p 78: © Timothy O'Rourke; p 83: © Timothy O'Rourke; p 84: © Rough Guides/Alamy; p 85, top: © Steve Vidler/eStock Photo; p 85, bottom: © Rough Guides/Alamy; p 86, top: © Timothy O'Rourke; p 86, bottom: © JTB Photo Communications, Inc./Alamy; p 87, top: © Jeff Greenberg; p 87, bottom: © James Marshall/Corbis; p 88: © Justin Guariglia/Corbis; p 89: © Joey Nigh/Corbis; p 90: © Timothy O'Rourke; p 91: © Arcaid/Alamy; p 92: © Timothy O'Rourke; p 96, top: © Timothy O'Rourke; p 96, bottom: © Timothy O'Rourke; p 97: © Timothy O'Rourke; p 98, top: © Timothy O'Rourke; p 98, bottom: © Timothy O'Rourke; p 99, top: © Timothy O'Rourke; p 99, bottom: © Timothy O'Rourke; p 100: © Greg Elms/Lonely Planet Images; p 101: © Larry Lilac/Alamy; p 102: © Timothy O'Rourke; p 103: © Timothy O'Rourke; p 104: © Timothy O'Rourke; p 107: © Atlantide Phototravel/Corbis; p 108, top: © Paul Hilton/epa/Corbis; p 108, bottom: © Terry Whittaker/Alamy; p 109, top: © Greg Elms/Lonely Planet Images; p 109, bottom: © Timothy O'Rourke; p 111, top: © Timothy O'Rourke; p 111, bottom: © Timothy O'Rourke; p 112: © Timothy O'Rourke; p 113: © Phil Weymouth/Lonely Planet Images; p 114: © Melvyn Longhurst/Alamy; p 115: © Timothy O'Rourke; p 116: © Timothy O'Rourke; p 120: © Timothy O'Rourke; p 121, top: © Timothy O'Rourke; p 121, bottom: © Timothy O'Rourke; p 122, top: © Greg Elms/Lonely Planet Images; p 122, bottom: © Jochen Tack/Alamy; p 123: © Timothy O'Rourke; p 124, top: © Timothy O'Rourke; p 124, bottom: © Massimo Pacifico/AGE Fotostock; p 125: © Rough Guides/Alamy; p 126: © Timothy O'Rourke; p 127: © Phil Weymouth/Lonely Planet Images; p 128: © Michael Kemp/Alamy; p 129: © JTB Photo Communications, Inc./Alamy; p 131, top: © Iain Masterton/Alamy; p 131, bottom: © Thomas Lehne/Alamy; p 132: © Melvyn Longhurst/Alamy; p 133, top: © P. Narayan/AGE Fotostock; p 133, bottom: © Macduff Everton/Corbis; p 134, top: © Timothy O'Rourke; p 134, bottom: © K. Westermann/Corbis; p 135: © P. Narayan/AGE Fotostock; p 137, bottom: © Bill Wassman/Corbis; p 138, top: © imagebroker/Alamy; p 138, bottom: © SCPhotos/Alamy; p 139: © Jean Pierre Amet/BelOmbra/Corbis; p 141, top: © Andrew Burke/Lonely Planet Images; p 141, bottom: © Melvyn Longhurst/Alamy; p 143, top: © Derek M. Allan; Travel Ink/Corbis; p 143, bottom: © James Davis Photography/Alamy; p 145: © Ian Trower/Alamy; p 146, top: © Timothy O'Rourke; p 146, bottom: © Timothy O'Rourke; p 147: © Werner Otto/AGE Fotostock